THE LIFE AND TIMES OF
CRAWFORD
GORDON
AND THE AVRO ARROW

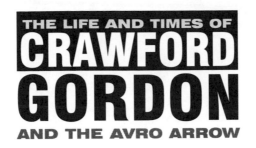

Arrow
Through
the
Heart

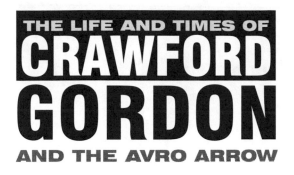

THE LIFE AND TIMES OF
CRAWFORD
GORDON
AND THE AVRO ARROW

Arrow Through the Heart

GREIG STEWART

AUTHOR OF
SHUTTING DOWN THE NATIONAL DREAM

 McGraw-Hill
Ryerson

Toronto Montréal New York Auckland Bogotá Caracas
Lisbon London Madrid Mexico Milan New Delhi San Juan
Singapore Sydney Tokyo

McGraw-Hill
Ryerson Limited

*A Subsidiary of The **McGraw·Hill** Companies*

300 Water Street
Whitby, Ontario
L1N 9B6
http://www.mcgrawhill.ca

ISBN: 0-07-560102-8
1 2 3 4 5 6 7 8 9 0   TRI   7 6 5 4 3 2 1 0 9 8

Care has been taken to trace ownership of copyright material contained in this text; however, the publisher will welcome any information that enables them to rectify any reference or credit for subsequent editions.

Canadian Cataloguing in Publication Data

Stewart, Greig
   An arrow through the heart: the life and times of Crawford Gordon and the Avro Arrow

Includes bibliographical references and index.
ISBN 0-07-560102-8

I. Gordon, Crawford, 1914-1967. 2. Chief executive officers — Canada — Biography. 3. A.V. Roe Canada — Biography. 4. Businessmen — Canada — Biography. I. Title.

HC112.5.G66S74 1998   338.092   C97-932430-0

Publisher: **Joan Homewood**
Production Coordinator: **Jennifer Burnell**
Editor: **Ron Edwards**
Electronic Page Composition: **Bookman Typesetting Co.**
Interior Design: **Dianna Little**
Cover Design: **Sharon Matthews**

Printed and bound in Canada

DEDICATION

This book is dedicated to the memory of J. Alan Hopper and Robert F. Thomas

ACKNOWLEDGEMENTS

*C*rawford Gordon's life and story was retold here based on a number of sources. I had letters, speeches and newspaper articles but most of all, I had people to talk to who remembered the man at a time in his life that was, in many cases, the time in their lives. These people made this story come to life after all these years. While dates, times and circumstances were occasionally a little vague, their memory of Crawford Gordon was as clear and unmovable as if they'd seen him but an hour before.

First and foremost, I'd like to thank the surviving immediate family members who gave of their time, private moments and recollections despite my many difficult and sometimes personal questions. Crawford Gordon III, the subject's son, supported this project from day one and was expressive, as only a son can be, on all aspects of his father's life. Crawford answered every one of my questions and provided invaluable information without hesitation. He also played a key role in opening a number of doors for me that would have otherwise been closed had I knocked on them myself. As well, his encouragement for this project is much appreciated.

Diana Gordon, his daughter, was equally as magnanimous in her willingness to provide information on the family and growing up in the Gordon household. Stephen Raphael, Crawford's stepson, welcomed me into his home over a humid weekend in Montreal, and revealed the difficult, painful details of the last years of Crawford's life. My gratitude also goes to Billie Gordon, Crawford's second wife, who willingly shared her experiences with him in the years after A.V. Roe Canada.

On a posthumous note, I'd like to thank Mary Gordon, Crawford's first wife, who spent many hours with me on an earlier book, sharing her memories of the man. Her gracious assistance is remembered. Also remembered is Fred Smye, Crawford's closest friend at A. V. Roe, who shared memories, views and thoughts of the tumultuous A. V. Roe Canada years.

Special thanks goes to those people whose job it is to help people like me find the answers to impossible questions yet do it so well. They include: Heather Clifford and Karen McNamara of the Inglis Corporation; Arden Phair, curator of the excellent St. Catharines museum; David Sobel, co-author of the book, *Working at Inglis;* Karen Teeple, curator at the City of Toronto archives; Fran Richardson, of the Appleby College Alumni Association; Tom Thompson of the McGill University Alumni Association; David Hahn whose father owned the John Inglis company and English Electric in the 1930s and 1940s; and Steve Payne, curator of the National Aviation Museum for photographs and access to the museum files.

I would also like to thank former employees of John Inglis, English Electric, Munitions and Supply, Canadian General Electric, A. V. Roe Canada and old friends of Crawford Gordon who gave of their time so that this story could be told. They include: Lou Cahill, Jim Gilmore, Jean Morley Taylor, Ron Adey, James C. Floyd, Gloria Collinson, Bill Dickie, Robert R. Robinson and George Mara.

As well, thanks to Dr. Gordon Bell, formerly of the Alcohol and Drug Addiction Research Foundation and Dr. Wilson Gasewicz, psychiatrist, who I called upon for information and analysis when it was required.

Irving Layton once said, "For my best moments, I need sunshine and tranquility and no obligations of any kind. Nobody to see, nobody to talk to, nobody to welcome. Nobody. I'm on my own, and I'm writing, and I'm happy." On a personal note I'd like to thank the following people who might not have been there beside me with pen in hand but were close by with their thoughts, interest and certainly their enthusiasm. These people let me alone and provided quiet encouragement during the completion of this project yet because of them, I didn't feel alone. They include: Judy Louise Doan, Joan Revie, Misty Pews, Carolyn Knowles, David Milne, Mike Townes, Marlene Fairbrother, Emma deVaal, Holly deVaal, Ian Paterson, Chrystelle Raphael, Indra Charma, Mary Ross Leckie, Keith Leckie, Ann and Larry Curley, Carol Collings, Elizabeth Suzuki Hosien, Margaret Gurr, Angela Kirton, Theresa, Nikki, Anthony and Franco at Picollo's, Cheryl Elizabeth Fielding, James Irwin Smith, Suzanne Brunelle, Dorothea Manson, Maria Iannone Burns, Garry Adams, Julie Rivett and Stu Rahmer.

Finally, I'd like to thank Joan Homewood, Erin Moore and Catherine Leek of McGraw–Hill Ryerson who had faith in this project and my editor Ron Edwards who brought the story to life.

Greig Stewart
Crossland, Ontario
Winter 1998

CONTENTS

Gloria Collinson
Sir Roy Dobson
Fred Smye
Jim Floyd
Audrey M. Underwood
Crawford Gordon's Children
Mary Gordon
Stephen Raphael
Gabrielle "Billie" Gordon

FOREWORD

I was shocked when I heard the sad circumstances of Crawford
Gordon's death in the mid-sixties. While I had not been as close
to Crawford as I was to my immediate boss, Fred Smye, who was the
man that really ran the aircraft side at Malton while Crawford was out
gobbling up additional companies in his bid to build up the A. V. Roe
Canada Ltd. empire, I had great respect and admiration for Crawford.

He was a man who could be both caring and ruthless, depending on
his assessment of a particular situation. He liked to gather around
him people he felt were "the best" in both competence and dedication to the job at hand. He would be extremely supportive of that
kind of effort. At the same time, he could be unforgiving if he
thought that anyone was falling short of his standards, as he demonstrated by "removing from office" a senior executive of the company
who had given a less-than-convincing briefing to government and
RCAF officials on a particular project in a meeting at which he was
present. There was no nonsense with Crawford: you were either good
or you were out! I have to say that I personally enjoyed that challenge. It certainly kept you on your toes!

Editor's Note: Jim Floyd arrived at A. V. Roe Canada from England in January
1946. His first project was to design a pure jet transport, the Avro Canada Jetliner, the aircraft which led North America into the jet age. He later headed up
the legendary design team that developed the CF-105 Avro Arrow, an aircraft so
ahead of its time, many front-line fighter aircraft can't match many of the Arrow's
capabilities even today. Floyd ended his career at Avro Aircraft as vice-president
of Engineering. He remains an icon in Canadian aviation.

I also experienced the compassionate side of his nature during the dark days of the Arrow project in 1955, when some members of the National Aeronautical Establishment, the Defence Research Board and the RCAF were continually sniping at Avro and particularly at Engineering. The result was endless re-evaluations, agonizing reappraisals and marathon time-consuming meetings just at the time we were trying to carry out the nearly impossible task of designing an aircraft that would meet the beyond-the-state-of-the-art RCAF operational requirement. Even today, with all of the advanced technology now available, that task would cause some loss of sleep to even the best of the modern design teams.

Eventually I became so "browned-off" with all of the nonsense that I snapped, and after a long conversation with my wife Irene, I sent Fred Smye a letter of resignation effective immediately. At around midnight on the following day, I got a phone call at our house in Port Credit. It was Crawford who was in England on business. Apparently Fred had informed him that I was about to quit. Crawford had already known how I was feeling about the relentless interference of the self-styled "experts," but he asked me to delay my decision until his return, since he considered that such a precipitous action would jeopardize the entire Arrow program and play right into the hands of the "knockers."

I finally agreed to do that, although I thought that his worries about "jeopardy" were overstated since I had organized the Engineering Division in a manner that there was always someone who could take my place without too much disruption of the programs under way. It was also obvious that some of the more persistent knockers would be glad to wave me goodbye!

Anyway, the next morning Fred Smye handed me an envelope containing tickets to Florida for Irene, our youngest son Michael and myself and said that Crawford had insisted that I take an overdue two weeks' vacation starting immediately to help shake off the doldrums, and that hopefully I would return in a better frame of mind and reconsider my decision. It was a generous gesture on Crawford's part and I finally wound down, said "to hell with the 'knockers'" and got on with the job.

When a few weeks later Crawford was giving me a friendly lecture on how not to let things get one down, I reminded him of an episode in April 1952 when we were having discussions with Howard Hughes about his interest in the C-102 Jetliner project. We were in RKO boss Walter Kane's Hollywood penthouse and in the middle of a conversation, Howard went off to the bathroom, presumably to obey the call of nature. When he had failed to reappear, about 90 minutes later, Crawford asked one of the staff to find out "if Howard has disappeared down the goddam hole." He was informed that "Mr. Hughes is on the telephone in the bathroom." After a further wait, Crawford finally became furious at these antics and stormed out of the penthouse. Apparently he was the only person ever to have walked out on Howard Hughes and here he was telling me how not to "snap" under duress!!

Some time after I left Malton following the Arrow cancellation to take a job in England, I was appalled to learn that Crawford had been thrown to the wolves by Sir Roy Dobson and had been blamed for all of the company's woes, and particularly, for his aggressive encounter with John Diefenbaker at the time of the cancellation. While his behaviour was certainly indiscreet, to say the least, and one does not embarrass the Prime Minister of Canada without some repercussions, Crawford's reaction was understandable in the circumstances. After all, Crawford was a complex human being, with all of the good and bad qualities of the species, and some of those who criticize him should look in the mirror now and then. It should be remembered that Crawford made an impact in many areas of Canadian life including his dedicated campaign in support of the Queensway General Hospital project, acknowledged on a plaque in its lobby.

He was certainly a great boss and friend to many people and did not deserve the sad and lonely end to his extraordinary and productive life. He was one of the last of Canada's great entrepreneurs.

James C. Floyd
Winter 1998

PROLOGUE*

*T*he tall, face-worn man poured himself yet another unnecessary drink this night in the living room of his New York apartment. Scotch again as it was most nights. For some Scotch is an easy drink, oil for the wheels of conversation or a quick painkiller to ease a day gone bad. For this man, nearly three decades of days gone bad had been made just a little easier with Scotland's finest in one hand and the company of a beautiful woman in the other. Both, however, had taken an obvious toll, ageing him well beyond his 52 years. Taking one more sip, the man rose from his chair, turned down Judy Garland on the hi-fi and shuffled, glass in hand, to the phone. Outside an early January snow had started to fall.

In Toronto, journalist and CBC commentator David A. Reynolds had just put his youngest son to bed for the night and was looking forward to a rare evening of reading and relaxing. Reynolds was a well-known, thoughtful writer who produced some of his best work in the 1950s, mostly in the area of military affairs, especially aviation. As he was leaving his son's room, the telephone rang.

"Hello?"
"Hello, Mr. Reynolds, this is the long-distance operator. Will you take a collect call from New York?"
"Of course," answered Reynolds, thinking it was one of his researchers.

---

*The scene depicted at the beginning and end of the Prologue is a composite of many calls Crawford Gordon made to journalists in his last days.

"Dave?" said the voice from New York. "This is Crawford Gordon."

* * * *

Crawford Gordon. His name still raises an eyebrow or two in Canada's business community some 30 years after his death. And so it should. The argument persists whether he was one of the greatest industrialists and business minds this country has ever produced, or whether he was nothing more than a canny political cowboy who herded the imagination of the entire country into his corral of schemes, ventures and moneymaking junkets. Unfortunately, because of his short life and because he did things quicker than most, the jury is still out. One thing for certain is that anyone who ever met Crawford Gordon, men and women alike, never forgot him.

"Gordon was a very blunt, fuck-you, sort of person," says former *Globe and Mail* aviation writer Jim Hornick. "Arrogant as hell in his operation of A.V. Roe Canada. And yet he had this kind of charm that just about dropped the pants off every lady he met. Unfortunately, he had no sense of self-preservation."[1] And it was this, in the end, that cost him it all. His companies, his fortune and eventually, his life.

For some months now I've tried to retrace the life steps of Crawford Gordon Jr. I've walked the tradition-soaked hallways and playing fields of Appleby College and McGill University and sat in the deserted assembly bays of what was once the legendary Avro Aircraft Company in Malton, Ontario. I've talked with family, friends, wives and lovers, adversaries and acquaintances. I have eaten where he had eaten and slept where he slept, all to gain some essence of the man — who he was, what he was, why he was.

But do you really learn about people from their footsteps? Can anyone really know another person simply from what they wrote, where they walked and who they talked to? Or does a biographer really just scramble to find as many pieces of the picture to at least begin this large puzzle in the hope that the pieces just might fit? And therein lies the dilemma. I have certainly not attempted by any means to paint a complete portrait of the man, but merely to reflect him through some of his life's experiences set against the times.

Such is this story of Crawford Gordon. Fragments of a 52-year-old life scattered across five decades and some 200 pages. He came from a family of bankers but the one thing he coveted — to become a director of a bank — eluded him. He would go out of his way to avoid small talk with his employees and yet travel to New York, the heart of the American financial community, to lecture the United States about how ignorant they were of Canada. He would strut by people he had known for years without as much as a hello, and yet he cancelled a golf tournament at a prestigious Toronto golf club because it had refused admittance to one of his employees, although Gordon had never met him, because he was black. When one of his business ventures turned sour, he bought a villa on the French Riviera complete with a Rolls Royce. When he was down to his last few dollars, he bought his second wife a diamond ring worth thousands. Some people found him coarse, and hard, but on more than one occasion, family members would find him at home in the evening, alone in the dark, listening to Judy Garland on the stereo with tears in his eyes. Crawford Gordon was strong and determined on the outside, alone but hating to be alone on the inside.

His early years held promise: he came from privilege, attended the finest schools, married his first love and had three wonderful kids. Things did come easy for him and he seemed to achieve success in half the time and at a younger age than most. At 21 he was comptroller of finance at Canadian General Electric; at 28, C.D. Howe's "Boy Wonder" at Munitions and Supply during the war; at 32, president of the English Electric Company; at 36, top man in the Department of Defence Production and then president of A. V. Roe Canada, the third largest company in Canada; at 40 he held directorships in nine of the largest corporations in Canada; at 52 he was dead.

Friends say he was driven but by what, to what and for what is the question. "I never had a definite plan or ambition,"[2] he would always say. Wealth and riches didn't interest him and power meant nothing to him. "To be in control," his son and stepson would say, "to always be in control,"[3] was most important to him.

Crawford Gordon had several of a number of things. He had three fathers — one natural and two surrogate. Of the latter, one was his former headmaster and the other, a British industrialist who would eventually disown him. He was also in love with three women — two he would marry and the third he would pursue for years. Their only similarity was their love for him. Over the years Crawford Gordon had four nicknames: "Pik" from his childhood, "Crotch" originating in his university years, "Boy Wonder" during his years with C. D. Howe and "Bash" from his later years, all distinct but each a reflection of the man during specific periods in his life.

For a businessman and industrialist, two curious characteristics typified the way he did business or, more accurately, the way he did *not* do business. The first concerned his colleagues. His past was rich in networks — the obvious fabric of business — from Appleby, to McGill to Munitions and Supply during the war. Yet he failed to utilize any one of his contacts or the loose network of friendships he developed. He didn't play by the rules of the business club because, by his own choice, he wasn't a member. Gordon's own club had a membership of one: himself. And the only rule of his club was: be alone, act alone. But he relied on himself for so long that it became hard to suddenly include others. By then, for Gordon, it became too late.

The second curious thing involved his adversaries. The more formidable his opponent, the more eager he was to rise to the occasion — and always with the most unorthodox results. This happened with Howard Hughes and John Diefenbaker, the two most formidable opponents of all. With Gordon the loose cannon, the resulting outcomes should have been otherwise, but for a different moment in time, one less glass of Scotch, one less ounce of impatience....

In many ways Crawford Gordon was like the project of his life, the ill-fated Avro Arrow aircraft. Both showed early promise but both met their demises much too soon, before we could get a look at how good they could have been. And yet, even though lost now for over 30 years, both live on in their own indomitable ways. They have become parts of the Canadian fabric to such a degree that they'll never go away.

"I'm one of those rankless people," Gordon once said. "I'm a dull sort of person. There's nothing really interesting about me."[4] In the end, you, the reader, will decide.

* * * *

"Crawford, I can't believe it, everyone thinks you're dead!"

"Yeah, well Dave, (cough!) I'm not dead. And if you think I've forgotten about those bastards in Ottawa and what they did to A.V. Roe and my Arrow, well I haven't. Now listen...."

"Where are you, Crawford ... what are you doing now?"

"I'm living (cough!) off Park Avenue, new wife and on my way back (cough!)."

"Well what do you want from me?"

"You know lots of press guys (cough!) and you were always good to me and A.V. Roe, so I wanted you to have the scoop on my new company. If you're still living in Weston, I think I have your address around here somewhere, I'll send you the details in a couple of days."

"And Dave? (cough!)"

"Yeah Crawford?"

"You know, I'm still gonna get that sonovabitch (cough!) Diefenbaker someday."

"Yeah, I believe you will," whispered Reynolds into the phone. "I believe you will...."

The next day, January 26, 1967, Crawford Gordon died in New York City. He had just turned 52.

Chapter One

THE EARLY YEARS (1912-36)

THE TITANIC

*A*s the White Star Line's flagship, the *Titanic*, steamed through the starlit, still night of April 14, 1912 to a destiny known only to God, a young Canadian woman from Winnipeg, Manitoba, heart filled with marital promise, slept peacefully in a first-class stateroom below deck. Ethel Flora Fortune, barely 28, was returning from England, a newly purchased wedding trousseau neatly folded in her steamer trunk. Her family was asleep close by. Her mother and father, Mark and Mary Fortune, her two sisters Alice and Mabel and her brother Mark had left Southampton bound for New York just six days before.

The voyage began as a joyous one for Ethel. She spent her time writing letters to friends and at afternoon teas and readings, evening dinners with souvenir menus and fine musical programs, all within the safe confines of a ship with the enviable reputation of being "unsinkable."

But not for long. At approximately 11:40 p.m. on that April evening, many passengers heard a noise they would later describe as "the tearing of calico." Soon after, members of the ship's crew ran down corridors ordering the all too familiar "All Hands on Deck." Few people knew it at the time, but the *Titanic* had hit an iceberg off the coast of Newfoundland. She would remain afloat for another two hours and 40 minutes.

Soon Ethel was woken by her father. She immediately dressed and headed for the deck where a steward gave her a life jacket and made her stand at the edge of the deck near a lifeboat. Her mother and two sisters joined her. Her father had disappeared and her 19-year-old brother was nowhere to be found.

Within minutes of striking the iceberg, the ship's six so-called water-tight compartments had been breached and the ship had started to list slightly. The ship's boilers had begun to hiss and the captain ordered the launching of distress rockets in the hope of attracting the attention of any nearby ships. Despite the fact that everyone now knew what was happening, there appeared to be no panic.[1]

> *I was in my cabin when the impact took place, Ethel would say to a rescuer days later, though unless the events which occurred after had happened, it was not so remarkable that I should have thought it out of the ordinary. I heard someone say the boat was going down and went up on deck to see what all the hubbub, which suddenly rose, was all about. We even were all assured that there was nothing to fear and that the ship had merely scraped an iceberg.*
>
> *When I heard the band playing, I thought it was all right and went back to my cabin and they began to lower the boats on the other side of the ship. I then tried to find my mother but was told by an officer that she was already in the boats. He hurried me to the side and I had to come down. The people in the boat caught me. As far as I could see, everything was carried out in first-class order and while we were in sight of the* Titanic *saw no disaster.*[2]

But disaster there was.

That night many survivors would experience sounds and sights that would stay with them for the rest of their days: the stupendous noise from inside the ship as she tipped on end, the detonation of the rockets, the hiss of the boilers. Nobody, however, forgot the most horrible of sounds: the cries of the hundreds that came from the ship as she sank. The cries of the drowning floating across the quiet sea turned the people in the lifeboats to tears. One survivor recalled that it reminded him of "one continuous wailing chant,"[3] like locusts on a midsummer night in the woods of his native Pennsylvania. The terrible sound lasted for 20, maybe 30, minutes gradually fading, as one after another succumbed to the cold water and slipped beneath the Atlantic. Then the silence.

Ethel never did see her father again and would later learn that he had gone down with the ship. But she did catch one last terrifying glimpse of her brother in the water, life jacket on, struggling to stay afloat. That sight, not surprisingly, would stay with her forever. She would learn that he finally became a victim of the sea.

The next morning Ethel, her mother and sisters in *Titanic* lifeboat number ten were pulled aboard the ship *Carpathia*.

Five days later Ethel's fiancé met his future bride fresh from the Halifax train. But she seemed older now, much older than the young lady full of love and hope and marital promise he had put on the train just a month before. Her experience on the *Titanic* had forever changed her. Some said it made her stronger while others felt she had become colder, more dominant and distant.

Within a year, in 1913, Ethel would marry her young suitor, Crawford Gordon, the first, the first of what would eventually become four Crawford Gordons, each of a different generation. Ethel's Crawford Gordon was the third of five children, whose family traced its roots back to eighteenth-century Scotland. Her husband had recently taken a position with the Canadian Bank of Commerce and his future looked bright. Although the Fortunes were more financially secure than the Gordons at the time, a girl from a good family, growing up and marrying a young man on the way up, could do worse in the Winnipeg society of the time. Their first born, appropriately named Crawford Gordon Jr., arrived on the chilly day after Christmas 1914. Two years later Ethel gave birth to another son, William, or Billy as he was known.

Roles and responsibilities within the Gordon family were clear and established very early on by Ethel. Crawford Sr. would manage the business of banking and Ethel would manage the business of raising the children. At times Crawford Sr. must have wondered what had happened on that *Titanic* night to his young bride. She never spoke of it but her domineering attitude and her iron-handed management of the Gordon household often startled him. Perhaps his mild, soft-mannered approach to things accentuated his wife's personality even more, made her appear even more domineering than she really was. Once, when Crawford Sr. was drinking more than Ethel thought he should, the message was simple: stop the drinking or I leave. He stopped his drinking.

"There was no question who wore the pants in that relationship," her grandson would recall years later. "It was Ethel."[4]

On November 1, 1920, Crawford Sr. was offered the chance to open a Canadian Bank of Commerce branch in Kingston, Jamaica. After the Great War, Canadian banks were expanding abroad and they proved excellent training grounds for eager young men with an eye for opportunity. So, with young Crawford and William in tow, Crawford Sr. and Ethel left for Jamaica to begin a five-year tenure.

Young Crawford's fair Winnipeg skin easily adapted to the Caribbean sun, so much so that he quickly became almost undistinguishable from the local kids. What did distinguish him, however, was his mother's insistence that he be enrolled in a private school. In the fall of 1920 Crawford entered Miss Beckwith's Private School in St. Andrew, Jamaica. The young man's journey to his future had formally begun.

In 1925 the Gordon family left Jamaica when Crawford's father was posted to the bank's head office at 25 King Street West in Toronto. The family took up residence in the Bloor Street\Mt. Pleasant Road area, close to the centre of the city where they would remain for six years.

THE APPLEBY BOY

On the western outskirts of the town of Oakville, some 25 miles west of Toronto and on the shore of Lake Ontario, lies Appleby College.

Bearing little resemblance to the bucolic college as first seen through the eyes of nine-year-old Crawford Gordon in the fall of 1925, today's Appleby is surrounded by suburban subdivisions. For young Crawford Gordon, fresh off the boat from the Caribbean, Appleby, the tranquil college by the lake, would be his home for the next six years. The school would give him his first challenges, both in illness and in good health, and would become the first of many institutions he threw himself into, yet later walked away from as if he'd never been there.

Appleby College began as a result of a conversation between Sir Edmund Walker and his son-in-law, John Guest, in the late fall of 1908. Although only in his mid-thirties, Guest had already made his mark in education as the first headmaster of the prep school of Upper Canada College in nearby Toronto. "Supposing you were to begin a boys' school of your own," asked Sir Edmund of Guest. "What would you give such a school? How would it be different from other schools?"[5]

Guest mused over the notion. He'd want a location in the country, far enough from the city to offer a sense of calm and space. That would be the central requirement. Then he'd keep the classes small so that each student — boys only, of course — would be guaranteed individual attention. Older boys would act as mentors and role models for the younger ones during the day, but at night the older students over the age of, say, 14 would have the chance to express themselves as maturing young men away from the bother of the youngsters. The school would have a strong church connection, to be sure. Good masters would be necessary, men who would combine discipline and sympathy with solid teaching ability. And this was just the type of school that opened on the quiet shores of Lake Ontario in the fall of 1911.

Crawford Gordon's father had returned to Canada from his five-year stint at the Canadian Bank of Commerce in Kingston, Jamaica in the summer of 1925 and the family settled into life in Toronto. For a time the tanned, healthy-looking Gordon was given the nickname "Pik," short for piccaninny from his Jamaica days. For Crawford's father and mother, there was no question that their sons would go to a private school. The question was which one. Crawford's father had originally wanted to send him to his Alma Mater, Ashbury College in Ottawa, but the school had been undergoing some financial difficulty and was threatened with closure. So Crawford Sr. turned to one of his colleagues at the bank for advice and the advice was to send Crawford to Appleby.

> *After giving very careful thought to the schooling of Crawford Jr.,* wrote Gordon Sr. *to his bank colleague, we have now decided to follow your recommendation and place him in Appleby. I am sure that it will provide all that we could wish for and we naturally want to put him into the very best hands. I realize it is a little late to put in his application but I do hope that you will be able to arrange to have him taken in. In our opinion he has had very good tuition at a private school [in Jamaica] where there are about 12 to 14 pupils and he is well advanced for his age (he will be 11 years old next December). Of course we realize that he will have to be graded when he gets into Appleby.*[6]

Not if, but when.

Glimpses of Appleby College are reproduced here from a school brochure printed in that period:

> *Character, intelligence and healthy bodies are Appleby's three main objectives for its boys. This task is assisted materially by the ideal conditions under which the school operates. The natural beauty of woods and lake unconsciously develops the aesthetic sense of an Appleby boy, which border our rolling playing fields. By a planned program of play, exercise and games, the boy develops in a healthful, happy environment.*
>
> *Careful attention is given to the work done by each boy in class. This is achieved by limiting the enrolment to 100 boarders and through small classes and a well-chosen staff.*
>
> *The finest traditions of fair play, honesty, loyalty and idealism are developed in the communal life of the boy. Worship is a normal and regular part of school life.*

All that is best in the experience and learning of the past is placed before each boy as inspiration and encouragement. He is led to exercise his own intelligence to choose the best, to establish a foundation for his own creative thinking and acting.[7]

The Appleby College that greeted Crawford Gordon Jr. in the fall of 1925 consisted of a scattering of buildings on the shore of Lake Ontario which included: the school house, an ivy covered building containing classrooms, offices, a library and the dining room; Powell's House, named after a former schoolmaster killed in the Great War, made up of dormitories and a workshop in the basement; the chapel, a church built in dedication to former students killed in the Great War; the hospital, with bedrooms and quarters for the resident nurse (a building Crawford would become all too well acquainted with in his tenure at Appleby); the gymnasium containing gymnastic apparatus and a stage for drama productions; and the covered hockey rink with a spectators gallery and a heated change room.

Discipline at Appleby was administered under what was known as the "house system." In charge of each house, or dorm, was a housemaster who was assisted by three or four resident masters, all entrusted with maintaining control. Prefects, or school police, were appointed from among the senior boys who, it was hoped by their influence and example, would maintain the traditions of the college.

In the classroom, every boy was expected to give strict attention to his work. The self-discipline required for the mastery of academic work was deemed to be sound preparation for the requirements demanded for the professions and business life. And that is exactly where Crawford Gordon, the Appleby Boy, was destined: business or the professions.

Outside the classroom, masters and boys were in constant association. In the dining hall, a master sat at the head of each table but rotated on a weekly basis to allow boys and masters to become better acquainted. Every effort was made by staff to encourage discussions on topics of current interest. Strict attention was paid to table manners, personal tidiness and neat and orderly rooms. Smoking was forbidden.

Subjects included English, Latin, French, Mathematics, Science, History and Geography specifically designed to prepare the boys for universities in Canada and the United States or for entrance into the Royal Military College, a very popular school for many Appleby Boys. Time was also set aside for music, singing, public speaking and debating as well as Bible study, current events and physical training.

The Appleby school year of 1925 was divided into three terms: autumn, spring and summer. Holidays included three weeks at Christmas, ten days at Easter and a long weekend at the end of each term. Boys were free to be with their parents every Sunday afternoon until evening chapel and leave was granted every third Sunday after morning service until 7:15 p.m.

Athletics were very important for an Appleby Boy. Once registered for school, every pupil was assigned to a squad of boys of similar age and size. Each squad created two teams operating under the supervision of two staff members. The focus was not upon the fine technical knowledge of a particular sport, but upon team play, from which the Appleby Boy was expected to reap the rewards derived from cooperation and to develop the true meaning of sportsmanship.

Physical training was mandatory and all boys 12 years of age or over were expected to become members of the Cadet Corps, which was affiliated with the Royal Regiment of Canada. With uniforms rented and supplied by the college, the Cadet Corps was intended to teach Appleby Boys self-control, discipline, poise and erectness of carriage.

The youngest boys received particular attention at Appleby. Each morning they were inspected by the school nurse and their activities were carefully supervised; great pains were taken to teach habits of personal cleanliness.

Non-classroom activities included the Dramatic Society, the Camera Club, the Literary Society, woodworking and a whole myriad of sports. A typical day for Appleby students was full, to say the least, by anyone's standards. Rising at 7:00 a.m., students were encouraged to study until breakfast at 8:00, followed by room inspection and chapel before classes started. Classes were typically from 9:00 a.m. until 3:00 p.m. with a half-hour for lunch. Athletics took place between 3:00 and 5:00, with the boys being expected to dress for supper at 5:30. After supper was set aside for studying, house prayers, milk and biscuits and an hour for personal recreation before lights out at 10:15 p.m. sharp. It was a regimen to discipline the undiscipline of youth.

A healthy, tanned 10-year-old Crawford Gordon Jr. walked through the gates of Appleby College in the fall of 1925 and immediately became an Appleby Boy under the watchful eye of headmaster and school founder, J.S.H. Guest. His first year at Appleby was quietly uneventful, a far cry from what lay ahead.

Although Crawford's parents and younger brother Billy remained in Ottawa and seldom visited, the elder Gordon sent a steady stream of letters to the school, a few to young Crawford, but most to Headmaster Guest. On some weekends Crawford would either take the train to visit his parents or stay with his mother's sister, Mrs. H.C. Hutton, on Forest Hill Road in central Toronto.

In the spring of 1927 Crawford's father was asked to become a member of the board of the college and readily accepted, allowing him to maintain an even closer contact with the school and his first son. School board directors in the 1920s played an advisory, non-interfering role in the running of school affairs, leaving the teaching and discipline entirely to the school administration. The elder Gordon found himself, both as school board member and parent, in the position of defending Appleby on occasion.

The report that you have heard about Appleby being a rich man's school, he wrote to a friend in Calgary, is something that was broadcasted a year or two ago, but I can assure you that before sending Crawford Jr. there I looked into this very carefully as we are not in a position to stand for any such training for our lad. The facts are that the tuition fee of $750

*per annum is just about the same, if not exactly the same, as
all other schools in and around Toronto, such as St. Andrew's,
T.C.S. etc. The extras are not very great and I would say off
hand that, including the various sundry articles such as gym
outfits, the odd pair of football trousers etc., that they would
not run more than $200. Their pocket money is 25 cents a
week and, not only do I consider their scholastic training far
better than the other schools', but I am really delighted with
the way the masters handle their sports. Were it not for the
fact that we were fully satisfied with the way in which Crawford was progressing, we would naturally have brought him
up to Ashbury School here.*[8]

For young Crawford, 1927 was a miserable year at Appleby. It was the
time when he would become almost as familiar with the school's
infirmary as he would with its playing fields and classrooms. During
a rare visit with his parents in Ottawa the previous October, he suffered fainting spells causing his father to write to Headmaster Guest
that his son appeared "quite pale, apparently getting over a cold," and
asked the headmaster to "keep a fatherly eye on him."[9] It would prove
to be an omen. Between January 1927 and February 1928, Crawford
got the measles (January), chicken pox (March), scarlet fever (December) and pleurisy (February). He was so sick that the only non-acad-
emic school activity he participated in was, curiously, violin lessons.

"It has naturally been a matter of great sorrow to ourselves to have
him knocked out in this way," his father would write of the time.[10]
Crawford spent the entire summer of 1928 convalescing at a cottage
on Blue Sky Lake near Ottawa. And yet despite his illnesses, he made
his academic year and actually won prizes for languages and profi-
ciency in general.

Almost as if he were determined to make up for lost time, Crawford
literally threw himself into all manner of school activities as the fall
term of 1928 began. He participated in literally everything he could
including boxing, tennis, badminton, basketball, golf, rugby, soccer,
hockey and track and field, excelling in tennis, golf and soccer. Crawford's abilities in tennis and golf would stay with him all his life. And

yet his parents still seldom visited or wrote to him, preferring instead to keep track of his activities through correspondence with the college's headmaster, John Guest. Right under their eyes, their first born was becoming a high achiever, but they didn't seem to notice, except when it came to matters of health.

> *As you are aware he is growing very rapidly, his father would write to Headmaster Guest, but on the other hand I noticed that he is keeping his weight up, which, considering the fact that he is apparently taking an active part in rugby, is to me a good sign. I would, however, appreciate it if you would have the doctor check him over thoroughly, examining his chest etc. and if you think it advisable, you might be able to persuade him to 'let up' a bit. His mother and myself would not have him know for anything that I have written you, as he is rather sensitive about his health and has assured us he is feeling fine, so I will leave it entirely in your hands to approach him in a way that will not indicate that you are concerned or that we know anything about it.[11]*

Although they rarely visited, Crawford's parents were pleased to have their son at Appleby. In May of 1929 they wrote to Headmaster Guest that they were planning to enrol their other son, Billy, in the college for the fall 1929 term, but that they had some financial concerns.

> *He [Billy] is ten years of age and is at present in junior form. Confidentially, the expense, however, of having two boys at boarding school is, naturally, one which we have to consider, and I am wondering what the arrangement is, if any, in the way of a reduction in fees where two brothers are attending the school at the same time.[12]*

Some satisfactory arrangement must have been reached for Billy enrolled at Appleby in the fall of that year.

All through the 1930 school term, Crawford continued to actively participate in sports at Appleby; in some he excelled, in others he was barely a participant. In rugby he played half-back and the school yearbook praised his work saying: "He played very well during the season and next year should be a first-class half. He did his best work on the line where his plunging was outstanding."[13] He continued on the track team in the one- and two-mile runs and even played goal on the 1930-31 school hockey team. In cricket he didn't fare as well, placing last on the team in runs, with a lowly score of nine.

Off the playing fields of Appleby, Crawford was just as busy. He joined the Cadet Corps and rose to the rank of section commander. He became a house prefect and house librarian which gave "considerable training in executive ability," and "by their influence and example, continue and strengthen the best traditions of the school."[14] He even found time to act in a play entitled *Le Voyage de Monsieur Perrichon*, the dialogue of which was entirely in French. Crawford was bilingual, and would later make sure his children learned French as well.

By October of 1930, 15-year-old Crawford had had enough of Appleby and was in a hurry to leave school and get a job. His worried father wrote to Headmaster Guest:

> From what I can see, Crawford's bent is towards commercial life and along the financial path, but it is naturally not our desire that he should take up work at too early an age. If all goes well, he should take his senior matriculation next June, at which time he will be 16 and a half years of age. He will then be too young to go into either the University of Toronto or McGill, particularly as he would not be residing at home and, therefore, his mother and myself would prefer to have him remain on at school for another year, during which time he and ourselves would have a further opportunity to judge as to the advisability of him following further his studies in an honours arts course. I take it from the conversation we had that your idea is that he should remain on at Appleby for another year....
>
> As you can possibly judge, Crawford has rather got an idea that he would like to start to work next fall, and I think he

has been influenced in this by the fact that a good many boys have left Appleby after taking their senior matriculation. He also has a notion that he would be further ahead in the long run by starting to work now than by staying on at school for another few years.

Headmaster Guest did talk Crawford into remaining at Appleby for another year with a further recommendation that he continue his "bent towards commercial life" and consider enrolling at either the University of Toronto or McGill University. Crawford's choice would be the latter.

In March 1931 Crawford Gordon Sr. was appointed manager of Canadian Bank of Commerce on Lombard Street in London, England, effective May 1. With both boys now at Appleby, the plan was to have Billy leave the school and travel with his father to England and to have his mother remain in Canada until Crawford had completed his senior matriculation in June.

"We in the banking world have to follow the orders given to us," he would write to Guest, "and, naturally, when a move such as this takes place, it would be out of the question for us to leave the little lad behind. It is a very attractive appointment...."[15]

Billy went to England with his father and enrolled in a private preparatory school in London and in June, Crawford went on to complete his exams for his senior matriculation. Of all the students in his graduating class who normally studied six subjects to graduate, Crawford carried an astounding 11 subjects, second in the entire school to one A.J. Little with 12. Carrying that many subjects allowed you your choice of virtually any university. His top subjects included Physics, English Composition, Algebra, Geometry, Trigonometry, Latin and French — unlikely subjects for a student with a "bent towards commercial life."

I can assure you that we are very much pleased with the way in which the boys were taken care of at Appleby, wrote an elated father to Guest, and fully satisfied with the education they have received in the hands of yourself and the masters

*of the school. We had hoped that Billy would follow in Craw-
ford's footsteps. As Crawford is returning to pursue his studies at McGill you will no doubt see him at Appleby
occasionally and he has already mentioned his desire to go up
there on your sports days, which indicates his attachment to
the school.*[16]

Crawford showed all the signs of being a high achiever at Appleby.
Despite the fact that his parents rarely wrote or visited him and losing a year to illness, he was very successful academically and participated in all manner of school activities. Some people would say that
when you're a high achiever and your parents aren't there to support
you, the message might be your achievements don't matter. Only
time would tell if this was the case with young Crawford. And the
first clue appeared soon after graduation.

Appleby would be the first to experience the phenomenon that when
Crawford Gordon was finished with something, he truly was just
that — finished. He would turn his back and walk away for good.
Where some would relish their schooldays and look back upon them
with affection, Crawford seldom referred to his time at Appleby and
would only talk about the school if someone asked. After graduating
he rarely corresponded with his mentor, Headmaster Guest.

In the late 1940s, in a puzzling move, while living in St. Catharines,
a short drive around the lake from Appleby, Crawford chose to send
his only son to Ridley College, an Appleby rival. When asked by his
son why he wasn't being sent to Appleby, Crawford replied, "They're
a bad patch," and said nothing more.[17]

THE McGILL MAN

The summer after graduating from Appleby College had 16-year-old
Crawford Gordon living with his parents and brother Bill at 52
North Gate, Regent's Park, London, England. His father's position
with the Canadian Bank of Commerce there opened the door for
young Gordon to work as a trainee/runner at the well-known stock-

broking firm of Kit Kat Aiken. In those days, a runner was little more than a glorified gofer but one who was entrusted with actually "running" stock certificates and documents between various offices within the company, or between various companies within the city.

Colleagues at the firm remember Gordon that summer as a rather cocky young man. One day one of his managers sought to teach the young man a lesson. "Gordon," he said, "Go down to the Bank of England and pick up the General Ledger." The General Ledger is a summary of the Bank of England's accounts, including all financial entries, and is never made available to anyone, let alone an unknown Canadian boy. When Gordon showed up at the bank, they laughed in his face. "Hey, I'm Crawford Gordon," he said, "And I'm from Kit Kat Aitkin and I want the General Ledger NOW!" Of course he didn't get the ledger, but that was his attitude in those days.[18]

Near the end of the summer job, Gordon was called into what was known as the "Partner's Room," which usually meant instant dismissal. When Gordon arrived, all the partners were there including the head of the firm, Lord Harding.

"You're a Canadian so you must know about these things," said Harding, handing Gordon a yo-yo. "Teach us what to do with this, this newfangled thing from America." And for the next two hours, one of Canada's future industrialists taught the board members of one of Great Britain's leading stockbrokers, how to "walk the dog" and do "round the world" with a yo-yo.[19]

In the fall Gordon returned to Canada to enter McGill University's School of Commerce.

Montreal in the 1930s was the cultural centre of Canada and a wide open city on a high. It was a challenge for anyone to find enough time to enjoy the city and what was happening. The Depression was there but it seemed less noticeable in Montreal with its entertainment — restaurants, bars, shows and lots of sin. It was a remarkable contrast to Toronto. Toronto was as quiet as Montreal was loud. Despite the power of the Catholic Church in Quebec and its ability to control a certain segment of the population in those days, everyone else partied in Montreal. The oasis in this sea of sin was McGill University and Crawford Gordon walked through its Roddick Gates as a freshman in the fall of 1931.

"The story of McGill," writes Stanley Frost, the university's historian, "is intertwined with that of Montreal itself."[20] Founded in 1821 on a bequest by James McGill, the university began as an all-male institution until women were admitted in 1884. The McGill University that greeted Crawford Gordon that fall of 1931 was a collection of some 60 buildings scattered across a 26-acre campus.

Although Gordon was one of 50 or so students registered in the university's School of Commerce, a little-known division of the Faculty of Arts and Science, McGill had already achieved an international reputation in medicine and the sciences. With a student enrolment of 3,661 and a staff of 551, the university's operating budget that year was a little over $2 million. But because this was the beginning of the Great Depression, McGill, like most other institutions, was operating under a program of austerity. So was Crawford Gordon. At a time when people were lucky to make $25 per month, Gordon's tuition for the year amounted to $150. The summer job in London had provided him with some money, but it was not long before he was donating blood to raise extra cash. And his choice of program caused him some initial problems as well.

Commerce students dealt in the area of money, recalls Tom Thompson of the university's alumni association, "and because of that, we were probably not well thought of at McGill in the 1930s."[21] That is, of course, unless you became a Zate.

Zeta PSI was one of 17 fraternities at McGill, none of which were officially recognized. Fraternities at McGill in those days were very elitist and very selective in whom they invited to become members. Fraternity members were usually the movers and shakers, the people doing things, the outgoing people very much involved in campus life.

Zates, in particular, had a reputation for heavy drinking and were largely rich kids whose parents had probably seen a $1,000 bill. For drunken Zates, a safe trip back to campus from a downtown bar was made possible courtesy of the Montreal police who knew the meaning of a $10 bill slipped under the driver's licence.

"The heroes in college," says Gordon's stepson Stephen Raphael, "then as now were the people who excelled in sports. The football captain could be a moron but would still be number one in many people's eyes. Because Crawford was popular and seen as a good athlete, he was voted most likely to succeed at Zate House."[22]

Gordon moved into Zate House at 3637 University Avenue on campus and immediately realized the obvious advantages of the location. It was close to the campus's Molson Stadium, and was within walking distance to one of Montreal's "red light" districts on De Bullion Street.

One time Gordon visited one of the bars on De Bullion Street, the kind that was cheap and open all night and ended up chatting up a woman. Little did he know the young woman "belonged" to the bartender and before he knew it, he was literally thrown out into the street. Back on campus he mentioned the incident to one of his Zate brothers who happened to be captain of the wrestling team. Next night the six-man wrestling team showed up at the bar, broke the offending bartender's arm and proceeded to trash the place. Nobody fooled with a brother Zate.

Crawford Gordon fell in love with Montreal during his years at McGill, a love affair that would bring him back to the city many times for both pleasure and business and, for a short time in the 1960s, it would be home.

Many of the activities in which he took part at Appleby, he would undertake again at McGill, including football, rugby and hockey. In 1932 he was a starring member of the school's junior football team which would go on to win the Canadian championship for the first time in the school's history. And, building on his dramatic experience at Appleby, he would perform for four straight years in a number of roles in the university's famous vaudeville show, the *Red and White Revue*, receiving some acclaim in the school newspaper. Not only did he perform on stage, he also worked behind the scenes as both program director and, not suprisingly, business manager for such long-forgotten productions as *Thirteenth Nightie, Heartthrobs* and *I Wanna Sing*.

There is no evidence he was active in politics in any way at McGill, where socialist debate sometimes flourished on the campus during the Depression. The 1936 McGill yearbook — his graduating year — listed his hobby as "week-ends," his pet peeve as "nine o'clocks" and his favourite expression as: "Let's go!" When each graduating student was asked to come up with a literary phrase that would best exemplify them as people, Gordon chose:

> *"Ah, make the most of what we yet may spend,*
> *Before we too into the dust descend...."*[23]

Gordon graduated from McGill University in 1936 with a Bachelor of Commerce degree. Years later he would readily recall three things from his university days in Montreal: his first affair with a married woman, being a Zate and his love for the city. The university's motto was "success through hard work," and it would not be long before its effect on its recent commerce graduate became apparent. And yet, he would leave McGill with almost the same ambivalence with which he left Appleby. The only contact that he would have with the university after graduation was sending a few hundred dollars to a building fund and to allow his name to appear on the alumni mailing list, but once. And as with Appleby, his son, Crawford III, would receive his business education at the University of Western Ontario. Diana Gordon recalled years later her father's dread that any of his children go to university, let alone his Alma Mater, McGill.

Chapter Two

FIRST CAREER MOVES
(1936-46)

CANADIAN GENERAL ELECTRIC

*A*fter graduating from McGill and taking the summer off, Crawford Gordon began work at the Canadian General Electric Company that fall of 1936.

Canadian General Electric can be traced to 1882 when two companies were founded: the Edison Electric Light Company of Hamilton, Ontario and the Thomson-Houston Electric Light Company of Montreal. The two merged six years later as the Canadian Edison Manufacturing Company and established a factory in Sherbrooke, Quebec to manufacture dynamos for generating electricity through a mechanical action. The Canadian General Electric Company was eventually created in 1892 from the merger of Edison General Electric Company, Edison Electric Light Company, the Toronto Construction and Electrical Supply Company and the Canadian General Electric Company. In addition to the head office and warehouse in Toronto, the company had plants in Peterborough, Hamilton and Sherbrooke, with branch stores in Halifax, Montreal, Winnipeg and Vancouver.

By 1921, due to a growing emphasis on electrical apparatus and appliances, the company concentrated on manufacturing transformers, electric boilers, large switchgear, substation equipment and appliances under the Hotpoint and General Electric names. By the time Crawford Gordon joined the company, the Depression had hit and profits had declined from $4.4 million in 1929 to just over

$600,000. Profits improved marginally through the rest of the Depression but failed to reach the plateau of the late twenties. As the economy improved and consumption increased, the company began producing more consumer goods, such as lamps, which made up a large portion of the sales volume.[1]

Twenty-one-year-old Crawford Gordon, fresh out of McGill, joined Canadian General Electric that fall and immediately went to work for the company's financial wizard, Harold Melvin Turner. Massachusetts-born Turner was a mechanical engineer when he started at CGE's Schenectady operation in 1921, but he soon joined the company's business-training program and became a specialist in cost analysis. In 1926 he was sent to Toronto to assist in the completion of a financial survey, ended up staying, took out his Canadian citizenship and became company comptroller in 1936, the same year that Gordon joined CGE.

"I was on special assignment for a while," Gordon would say in a rare interview years later. "Then I went to the head office in Schenectady for a two-year training course."[2] But before leaving for Schenectady, there was a matter that needed attending to: how to get a young Toronto woman by the name of Mary Tierney to marry him?

Mary Tierney was just 20 years old the first time she met Crawford Gordon in the fall of 1936. Born on May 29, 1916, she was the second of two daughters of Josephene and John Tierney of London, Ontario. Her father was a marketing man with British-American Oil (now PetroCanada). The Tierneys didn't have a lot of money, but what they had they spent freely on Mary and her sister Doris.

"My mother always had a circle of good female friends," recalls Mary's daughter Diana. "Her parents were simple folk. The Tierneys had this little house and Mom was born on the kitchen table for gosh sake. I can remember grandmother baking pies from fruit grown in the backyard and great sumptuous Sunday dinners. My Gordon grandparents seemed so grand compared to the Tierneys, but whatever it took financially for Mom to participate in social activities, it was done."[3]

As happy as the Tierney household was, it was not free from tragedy. A year after she was married, Doris would die from a brain haemorrhage. She was just 24.

Mary was able to attend a private school, St. Clements, where she met her lifelong friend Frances, who would later become Frances Lumbers, wife of Len Lumbers, former president of the Argonaut Football Club and later Crawford Gordon's closest friend. Mary excelled at St. Clements, had a very active social life, loved movies, track and field and at the end of Grade 12, became a debutante. The family moved to Toronto in the 1930s, and it was common for young women to make their formal entrance into society (known as "coming out") by attending socials and parties which announced to potential young suitors that they were available for courtship.

Mary would never find herself short of suitors, before, during and after her marriage, yet she would remain as "faithful as bark on a tree to Crawford."[4] During her life she would be pursued by a young George Hees (later a prominent Tory Cabinet minister under Diefenbaker) and the not so young entertainer Danny Kaye.

Mary Tierney first set eyes on Crawford Gordon in the summer of 1936 at a social and was immediately warned by a friend to "stay away from that guy 'cause he's a real womanizer."[5] Despite being engaged to be married by the spring of 1937, Mary would soon come face to face with, and fall victim to, Gordon's charm and determination. The engagement not withstanding, Gordon had somehow found out she lived on Balmoral Avenue in Toronto, got her phone number and called her up to ask for a date.

"Are you free next Saturday?" he asked.
"Sorry, I'm busy that night," was the reply.
"Well how about Sunday?" he asked.
"Sorry, busy then too," was the reply.
"Well then, how about Monday?"
"No, can't then either."
"Tuesday?"
"Sorry."

"Well then, how about Wednesday?" he asked again, his impatience showing.

"Yes, that would be fine, Wednesday would be fine," she replied.

"Great, then I'll see you Wednesday. Oh, and Mary?"

"Yes?"

"Don't plan anything for the next two weeks or so because you'll be seeing me every night!" he declared.[6]

"He wouldn't leave me alone," Mary would recall years later. "From the first time we met, he wouldn't let up on me. He was so, so irresistible … I liked his style."[7] Mary would soon see Gordon's "style" in action. Just prior to their first date, Gordon was dining with friends at the Imperial Room of the Royal York Hotel in Toronto when who should walk in but Mary and her fiancé. Desperate to get her attention, Gordon sent a rose to her table. Nothing happened. He then sent another rose. Again, nothing happened. He then started throwing dinner rolls at her from across the room. Crawford and Mary were married two weeks later, in September 1937, just in time for him to report for duty to Schenectady with Canadian General Electric. They honeymooned at Murray Bay (La Malbaie) resort, 150 km. east of Quebec City.

"All my mother ever wanted," recalls Gordon's son, "was to be happy and have a nice family. She was nothing short of a caring mother, a supportive wife and always had a pleasant disposition. To the day she died she never said a negative word about my father."[8] In many ways Mary would end up living the line from her favourite song from *Showboat*, "Can't help loving that man of mine.…" She was not alone.

Mary spent some time in Schenectady before setting up house in Toronto at 1 Kilbarry Road in South Rosedale. Mary and Crawford would have three children: Crawford III, born August 29, 1938 in Toronto; Cynthia Ann, born November 20, 1941 in Montreal; and Diana Mary, born March 4, 1944 in Toronto.

In Schenectady Gordon got an unexpected lesson on how business was done in the province of Quebec, a lesson he would put to use in his later years. One day Gordon got a visit from a monsignor, who came into his office, blessed him and said, "It has come to my knowledge that you have submitted a bid for turbines to be supplied to a particular utility in Quebec." The government of Quebec had tendered a project and CGE had submitted a bid. "Technically," the monsignor continued, "I believe your bid is fine — it's what we want. The only thing wrong is the price; it's too low." Gordon sat and listened, looking quite perplexed. "The price should be increased," said the monsignor, "and if it is, you'll get the contract. Now, with this higher profit margin, you may very well want to use it to make a contribution to the Catholic Church in Quebec and if you do, God would look favourably on you."[9]

Gordon naturally raised the price, the contract was awarded, the contribution was made and the young man got an early lesson on how things worked in Quebec in those days.[10]

"When I came back to Canada," Gordon would say later, "I was put on the internal auditing staff. That embraced a lot of jobs — market research and production costs and profits."[11] For a young man in a hurry, being on the audit staff at CGE held little excitement. Internal auditors make sure all the systems and controls in a company are sound and defensible, without loopholes, to ensure no opportunity for malpractice; it's an accounting function, and not very glamorous for an ambitious young man.

With the coming of the Second World War, Gordon was still on the auditing staff and still reporting to Hal Turner. Not interested in being in uniform but wanting to be closer to the action and the excitement (he was barely 26), stories began to drift out of Ottawa about this incredible Cabinet minister, C.D. Howe and what his newly created Munitions and Supply ministry was doing for the war effort. Gordon's own company was now making electrical equipment to supply other industries which were expanding to meet their wartime commitments and was even considering moving into armaments and munitions. But that wasn't enough for Crawford Gordon.

"Pack your bags Mary," he said to his young wife in July 1942, "We're going to Ottawa."

C.D. HOWE AND MUNITIONS AND SUPPLY

Canada declared war on Germany on September 9, 1939, and exactly seven months later, on April 9, 1940, Prime Minister Mackenzie King appointed his 58-year-old transportation minister C.D. Howe to the "largest single job of his career. On that day he became minister of Munitions and Supply, the new government department formed to steer Canada into full war production."[12]

Much has been written about Clarence Decatur Howe, who some consider to be "the greatest Canadian ever."[13] But if one is to understand the make-up of Crawford Gordon, one has to understand the make-up of the man who influenced him more than anyone in his life. For Howe, personality and management style were one and the same.

"He was very different from the old WASP elites that ruled Toronto and Montreal," writes Peter C. Newman in his excellent work, *The Canadian Establishment*, "whose members were British in their orientation, turning towards Government House, the Crown, and the Empire for guidance. Howe was middle class, self-made, a tough, American get-up-and-go engineering type. The dollar-a-year men who came to aid in the war effort had grown up with Hollywood movies, the first generation to do so. They were in love with the American style of easy-going brashness, the 'get things done without a lot of stuffy nonsense' attitude that Howe so perfectly epitomized."[14]

"Howe's administrative style was established early," add William Kilbourne and Robert Bothwell in their biography of him. "When he had picked the man he wanted to run an enterprise, he delegated near total responsibility to him. He expected him to take the initiative and backed him with absolute trust and support unless and until he found his confidence misplaced."[15] A colleague from those days recalls once being put to just such a test in Howe's office. It seemed a wartime company under Howe's jurisdiction in Quebec had submitted a request for $2.5 million worth of machine tools which they said was going to be used for war production. Howe's colleague, however, had visited the plant and came back convinced the company had ordered the equipment to produce furniture after the war.

The minister, under some pressure from some Quebec senators to ignore the situation, called the young man into his office.

"Are you prepared to stand behind what you say?" he asked.

"Yes sir," was the nervous reply.

"Then that's fine with me." answered the minister. End of discussion.[16]

What was not lost on the people around him was Howe's decision-making ability. "Once it's done," he used to say, "don't second-guess yourself. Never turn around." He had the ability to comprehend quickly and pick the guts out of a decision. Tough, cold, but always friendly.[17]

"Howe loved the personal relationship of leader to his men," write Howe biographers Kilbourne and Bothwell, "and in particular the dual roles of crusty demanding boss and solicitous amicable father.... The main point was that Howe was loyal to his people, loyal to a fault; they knew it and responded with a commitment and a standard of performance that often nobody thought they had in them. And the most unlikely men managed to work well together out of love or fear of their boss."[18] When a somewhat nervous employee once asked Howe, "What are your instructions, C.D.?" Howe calmly replied, "I never give instructions, I just give responsibilities."[19]

Clarence Decatur Howe was born in Waltham, Massachusetts in 1886, and graduated from the Massachusetts Institute of Technology (MIT) with an engineering degree in 1907 at age 21. After teaching at Dalhousie University in Halifax, Nova Scotia for five years, he moved to Port Arthur, Ontario (now Thunder Bay) where he soon established his own engineering firm which, over the next 15 years, built grain storage facilities in harbours across Canada and as far away as Argentina.

In 1933, his friend Vincent Massey, then president of the National Liberal Federation, convinced Howe to run as a Liberal candidate in the next federal election in 1935. He was elected and was promptly appointed minister of Canals and Railways. He then went on to become minister of Transportation, establishing the Canadian

Broadcasting Corporation (1936) and his personal favourite, Trans Canada Airlines (now Air Canada) in 1937. By 1940 he was set to transform the Canadian economy.

Howe's critics have called him all manner of things, but ideologically he was difficult to pin down. "The fact is," comments John Deutsch, a former wartime Ottawa mandarin, "C.D. didn't know a policy when he saw one. He knew how to run a railroad, how to make the thing go ... but *why* you had a railroad, that is a question he did not ask. He never had a decisive input in general policy matters. Someone responsible would tell him: 'This is what we need,' and he went and did it. He was an operating executive ... one of the greatest this country has ever had."[20]

"He looks and acts exactly what he is," writes biographer Leslie Roberts, "a stocky, candid, unpretentious 'engineering-type' executive who has become so accustomed to making the right decisions that he has never had to cultivate the slightest bit of side, put on the slightest bit of front or refrain from saying exactly what he wants to say. He is strictly an ad hoc man with little time or taste for abstract thought."[21]

Even Howe's American friends were startled on occasion by his "blunt talk, uninhibited by diplomatic niceties."[22] And yet in the last summer before the war, Crawford Gordon had not yet heard of C.D. Howe, the man who would soon become the only mentor he ever had, or ever wanted.

The idea that Canada would soon be at war was a very difficult thing for most Canadians to imagine even as late as the summer of 1939. Prime Minister Mackenzie King was completely convinced that war could be avoided, and after his well-known 1935 tour of Europe that included a personal audience with Hitler, King had returned to Canada and declared that a world war was remote and that the danger of an attack on Canada was "minor in degree and second hand in origin."[23] King was not alone in his thinking. Since losing over 60,000 young Canadian men in the First World War, the country had been in retreat from just about anything to do with the military, so much so that Canada's army, navy and flying corps were totally understaffed and underequipped to such a degree that one military historian wrote our forces had reached the "nadir of their neglect."[24]

Under pressure from some Cabinet members who opposed this naive isolationist view, the government quietly set up an agency in the summer of 1939 called the Defence Purchasing Board, later followed by the War Supply Board, whose functions were to basically begin, tentatively, to re-equip the country's armed forces. And this, despite the fact that the country had never undertaken such a venture.

And then came Dunkirk in June 1940, and suddenly Great Britain — until that point Canada's main source of military supply — found itself in the reverse position of coming to Canada for aid. But the Canadian warehouse was empty, defended by an army that had no equipment, an air corps that had no aircraft and a navy that had no ships.

Many Canadian historians feel that Mackenzie King's conception of the national effort during those early years of the war was his fear of imposing conscription to raise an army to fight overseas and the adverse effects conscription would have, not only on the country's unity but his party's chance of winning the next election. To King, Canada's contribution to winning the war was the development of a national war industry.[25]

And the job of setting up this war industry fell upon Howe.

But even a man of C.D. Howe's stature could not run Canada's war effort by himself. So he telephoned every part of the country, recruiting anybody who knew how to run a business and who combined common sense and determination with an absolute refusal to believe that nothing was impossible. The calls were answered from Halifax to Victoria; 1,000 men were willing to come to Ottawa for the duration for a dollar a year and the prestige of becoming part of an exclusive club known later as "Howe's Boys."

There was plenty to choose from, men mostly in their late thirties or forties, just over military age and just one or two steps below president in their own individual corporations: E.P. Taylor, H.R. Macmillan, John David Eaton, H.J. Symington and many more — the future Who's Who of Canadian business. Under normal circumstances, the government could not have afforded any of them, but the magnetism of the war drew them to Ottawa while their firms continued to pick up their salaries as a patriotic gesture.[26] Crawford Gordon became one of Howe's Boys.

Arriving in Ottawa, Howe immediately assigned Gordon to work for the strong man of Munitions and Supply, Harry J. Carmichael. Carmichael had worked for McKinnon Industries in St. Catharines before it was taken over by General Motors in 1929. Carmichael understood things like production technology and mass production techniques, valuable in wartime, and Howe quickly made him head of the Department's Production Branch, responsible for all aspects of wartime production; aircraft, motorized transport, vehicles and munitions. Where Howe was the czar in the Canadian Cabinet, Carmichael was the demi-czar to Howe.

Gordon began working for Harry Carmichael in Munitions and Supply set up in temporary office facilities near the Parliament buildings on Wellington Street. He took on with a relish every assignment, large or small, menial or great, that came his way. Being Carmichael's number one boy, Gordon's primary function was to observe, monitor and provide assistance to many of the country's companies working to convert to wartime production. He oversaw assembly lines, production schedules and troubleshooting at plants and factories from Halifax to Victoria. And while most of his colleagues roved around the halls at Wellington Street during those hectic wartime years, Crawford ran. No assignment was too small, every task might change the course of the war and Gordon took it as a personal challenge to complete any job ahead of what was already a tight deadline.

"Crawford worshipped C.D. Howe," recalls Mary Gordon, "and wanted more than anything the chance to work for him."[27] Crawford, Mary, Crawford Jr. and newborn Cynthia moved from Toronto to Ottawa, taking up residence near Lansdowne Park in the city's south end. Cynthia had been born on November 29, 1941, in Montreal and would have her father's stubborness, a trait that would keep the two more apart than together over the years. Crawford's workplace every day, night and weekend was Munitions and Supply's head-quarters at the Number One Temporary Building on the cliffs above the Ottawa River.

It's no wonder then, that within two weeks of his arrival in Ottawa, he had his label, Howe's "Boy Wonder." To Gordon, the "Boy Wonder" label never seemed to bother him, he would do anything without question or hesitation to please the Minister. Gordon had found his mentor in Howe, the only one he would ever have, or ever care to have and would admit on a number of occasions over the years that everything he learned about running things, he learned from the Minster of Everything, C.D. Howe.

> *For many of the dollar-a-year men, Second World War Howe was to be the most creative season of their professional lives. Their innovative talents flourished as they learned to extend the boundaries of their self-reliance, to manage the world at large, without having to copy or feel inferior to the British or Americans.... [Howe] taught them an important insight: that knowledge is power. In first reviving, then operating, a diverse economy flung across an unlikely hunk of geography, Howe's protégés deliberately set out to learn where all the important pieces were; who counted and who didn't, how to deal with each other, with Cabinet ministers and with the political system.... It was this network of connections and interconnections between business and government ... that became the Canadian Establishment [of post-war Canada].... When these dollar-a-year men fanned out at the close of the Second World War to run the nation they had helped to create, the attitudes, the working methods, and the business ethic they took with them determined the country's economic and political course for the next three decades.*[28]

And these men learned other lessons as well, as clear and basic as the man who taught them:

• Manage by delegating responsibilities.

• Give a man his job and stay the hell out of his way.

- Secure your source of supply by whatever means to ensure continued production.

- Reduce your dependence on others for supply.

C.D. Howe, his dollar-a-year men and the war — never in Canada's history had a combination clicked with such outstanding results even by today's standards. Through 28 Crown corporations and a number of other company conversions, Canada's defence output grew so fast that by 1943 we stood fourth among the Allied nations in industrial output, behind only the United States, Britain and Russia.

For the ministry, 1941 had been the year to plan, construct facilities and convert industrial plants to war production, which began in earnest the following year. By 1943 war-related industries were employing over a million men and women to complement the other million in uniform. The country's GNP had gone from $5 billion in 1939 to an astounding $12 billion. Munitions and Supply's annual budget alone was $1.365 million.

By 1944 the country had produced almost 11,000 different types of aircraft, nearly 600 ships, 500,000 transport vehicles, 31,000 armoured vehicles and 83,000 pieces of artillery. "Never again," said the minister in 1943, "will there be any doubt that Canada can manufacture anything that can be manufactured elsewhere."[29]

The dollar-a-year men always considered themselves grossly overworked considering their lives before the war, but what came out of the experience was a great sense of comradeship and a terrific binding together of people in common cause. "Eating lunch and often dinner with the same group for five years produced in the participants … a consensus about the kind of country they wanted after the war, the sort of business practices they believed in, [and] early glimmerings that Toronto and Montreal were not the only commercial centres in Canada that mattered. They began to exchange confidences, to sponsor one another for club memberships, to share perceptions and ambitions. It was an enduring trust and … no badge of honour carried more prestige than the phrase: "I put in time under

CD."[30] A friend of Winston Churchill's said of C.D. Howe, "But for him the war would have been lost."[31]

SIR ROY DOBSON AND HIS LITTLE EMPIRE IN CANADA

By the wartime summer of 1943, Sir Roy Hardy Dobson of the massive A.V. Roe Aircraft Company in Manchester, England was in need of a holiday. "Dobbie," as he was know to those out of earshot, was the managing director of the Roe operation which had given birth to such famous aircraft as the Anson, the Hurricane, the Tempest, the Whitley and most recently, a redesigned version of the heavy Manchester bomber known as the Lancaster.

For nearly two years now, the Victory Aircraft company in Malton, Ontario had been tooling up to build the Lancaster under licence and expected to have the first plane ready for delivery by August of 1943, months ahead of schedule. Victory Aircraft, formerly known as National Steel Car, had been "nationalized" by C.D. Howe's Department of Munitions and Supply and had become a Crown corporation with the specific purpose of producing the Lancaster bomber for the Allied war effort.

Dobson was well known in the aircraft business at the time, typical of so many British "pencil behind the ear" production managers of the era, and up-from-the-workbench type who never forgot where they came from, teethed and hardened by the rigours of early twentieth century life. To those who worked for him, he could be both irascible and charming, instilling both fear and affection at the same time, making assembly bay workers feel like royalty and reducing hardened line managers to tears. A father figure to some, a friend to a select few, a formidable force to all.

Since January 1942, stories had been drifting across the Atlantic about the incredible progress the Canadian plant was making producing the Lancaster. The Victory Aircraft people claimed they could produce one plane every six days, two days faster than the British could do at the Manchester plant. For Dobson, his war effort thus far had aged him well beyond his 43 years, so when a friend suggested a visit to Canada to see first-hand what was really going on, Dobson reluctantly agreed to the trip but only under the guise of a working holiday.

Hoping to arrive at Malton for the roll-out of the first Canadian-built Lancaster, Dobson missed it by a full two weeks. "Damn," he would say later, "I didn't expect the buggers to produce their first plane until next year!"[32] Dobson's interest in Canada, to say the least, had been aroused.

Sir Roy Dobson had been quite surprised at missing the roll-out of the first Lancaster at Victory Aircraft that August of 1943, so surprised that he decided to stay in Canada a few weeks to get a closer look at Canada's war industry. A typical English bulldog type, Dobson was not unlike many of the aircraft with which his company had become associated: powerful, rugged, reliable, hard to bring down and a disposition to be reckoned with. Ruddy faced and blustery at times, making a friend or enemy just about every time he opened his mouth, Dobson was a native of Lancashire in Northern England which, legend has it, was said to breed some of the toughest businessmen in the world.

Around Manchester's aircraft factories, Dobson was known as a "real bloody character"[33] who, as another legend has it, for over 30 years had been firing department heads on a Friday night, yet expecting them to be back at their desks on the Monday. Comfortable with a language so colourful at times, even some labour leaders blanched. Born in the village of Hortsforth, not far from Manchester on Sept. 27, 1891, Dobson went to work for the pioneering British aviator Alliot Verdon Roe at his A.V. Roe and Company as a draftsman in 1914, working his way up to works manager in five years.

Always referring to himself as "an aircraft man," Dobson took the blue collar off for good after the First World War, but insisted on keeping as close to the assembly bay floor as possible. A Dobson trait was that whenever his company got a contract, he insisted on tight delivery dates and was constantly all over his staff and workers to keep on schedule. One Canadian visitor recalls touring the A.V. Roe facility during the Second World War and feeling it was run like a "prison farm," with Dobson running about barking orders at every opportunity and staff standing stiffly to attention every time he passed by.[34] But in quiet conversation with friends, he would admit that he didn't mean half of what he said.

True or not, as with most individuals with character, Dobson had immense personal charm. He could make a woman on the plant floor feel like a movie star, and spend hours in personal conversation with an assembly line riveter. And he was on a first-name basis with both. By 1945, Dobson and his aircraft team at Roe had been responsible for 180 different aircraft types, but it was his work with the Lancaster bomber in the early days of the Second World War for which he was best known.

Shortly before the war, A.V. Roe Ltd. had entered the heavy bomber field with an aircraft known as the 679 Manchester, powered by two Rolls Royce Vulture engines and carrying a heavy payload. The aircraft turned out to be too heavy, the engines too sluggish and it never came close to the original performance the British Air ministry had hoped for.

A.V. Roe's designers went back to work and felt the solution lay in a four-engined aircraft, powered by Rolls Royce Merlin engines, designed for smaller and lighter Spitfire and Hurricane fighter aircraft. However, two problems lay ahead. When Dobson and his team asked permission from the Air ministry to redesign the original Manchester to fit the Merlin engines, it was denied, due in large part because the government had already invested heavily in the Vulture engine design. Dobson then turned to his friend Lord Beaverbrook, the Canadian-born minister of Aircraft Production, to let him have four Rolls Royce Merlins and to fund the redesign of the Manchester to fit them.

"No way," said Beaverbrook.
"Well, what about the engines?" asked Dobson.
"Go dig for them," was the reply.[35]

Dobson then turned to another friend, Lord Hives, head of Rolls Royce and "borrowed" four Merlin engines. With some modification, the redesigned Manchester, now called the Lancaster, was ready for test flight before an astounded group of RAF officials on January 9, 1941.

"And just where did you get those engines?" demanded Lord Beaverbrook.
"I dug for them," answered Dobson.[36]

The Lancaster was a spectacular performer. It was able to outfly the famous Hurricane fighter on the flat and became, according to Sir Arthur Harris, chief of Bomber Command, "the greatest single factor in winning the war."[37] The British Air ministry, a little less enthusiastic, begrudgingly admitted: "Although we must admit that the bomber has a remarkable performance, we cannot but deplore the methods by which it was obtained."[38]

When C.D. Howe heard that Sir Roy Dobson was planning to stay in Canada for a few days, he asked his director general of Aircraft Production, Ralph Bell, to show Dobson around and let the old man see whatever he wanted. Bell then passed the assignment on to his assistant, a young 27-year-old from Hamilton, Ontario named Frederick Timothy Smye. Smye was another of Howe's Boys, "men", writes Peter C. Newman, "full of ginger and ambition, set on getting ahead, not burdened with the inner conflicts people who grew up earlier and later endured."[39]

Eager to avoid military service during the war, Smye had talked his father-in-law, J.B. Carswell, into getting him a job, any job, with Munitions and Supply. He ended up working with Ralph Bell, Howe's Aircraft Production chief. Freely admitting he "knew bugger all about airplanes,"[40] Smye made up for his lack of technical skill with intelligence, salesmanship and optimism. Smye did all manner of jobs for Bell during the war and did them with heartfelt enthusiasm. A former colleague recalls that he "was a very clever fellow. Not that experienced, but did quite well with what he had."[41] Former aviation writer Jim Hornick adds, "Smye would have made one hell of a life insurance or shoe salesman. He was absolutely full of shit."[42]

Full of shit or not, Sir Roy Dobson was happy to have Smye to show him around the aviation industry in Canada that wartime summer. One of the first people Smye introduced him to was the Minister of Everything, C.D. Howe. Dobson and Howe were men of similar physical and emotional stature, speaking a common language separated only by accent; they understood that a handshake was as good as a deal and often better than a contract.

Over cigars and brandy in Dobson's hotel room in the Château Laurier in early September 1943, Howe talked about his vision of a postwar Canada and his hope of keeping unemployment down, but lamented over what he was going to do with all the excess industrial space in the country once the war had wound down. Still full of intrigue at what he had seen at Victory Aircraft, Dobson pulled out a cigarette package and began to sketch a proposal for Howe on his idea for taking over the Victory operation once the war was over. The two men "dickered in a minor way without coming to any agreement but Howe said, 'Think about it, Dobbie, and come back and see me in a week or so.'"[43]

"It opened my eyes, I'll tell you," recalled Dobson years later. "If these so-and-sos can do this during a war, what can't they do after. One thing this country would need is an aircraft industry of its own — design and development, not just assembling somebody else's stuff. And yet, it seemed to me that it might be lacking the finer engineering developments and things like aircraft engines and so on. And I couldn't possibly imagine a nation with this sort of potential carrying on without demanding, not just asking or thinking about, but demanding, its own aircraft, its own aircraft industry, its own engine industry and indeed, a lot of other industries too. But, of course, I was an aircraft man at the time and I said: 'All right that's my field. I'm going to have a go at it.'"[44]

To Fred Smye, he was more candid. "You know, Freddie," he would say on more than one occasion, "I used to dream of a little empire in Canada." Leaving Fred Smye, his new young charge, to keep an eye on things for him in Canada, Dobson returned to England in late September 1943. His "little empire in Canada" would have to wait for two more years.

Mackenzie King's government began debate on the winding down of Canada's war industry. The war in both Europe and the Pacific had finally started to turn in favour of the Allies and C.D. Howe felt that when the war finally ended, "there need be no fear of unemployment of those willing and able to work … a surprising number of war plants can be converted without difficulty. Many new types of production that have been organized for war can be continued for peace."[45]

The Cabinet agreed that a new type of organization was necessary to reconvert Canada's war industry. The new department was named Reconstruction and Supply and C. D. Howe, not surprisingly, became its minister. It was almost an exact copy of Munitions and Supply with a smaller budget, but with all the power and with the additional responsibilities of scientific research and jurisdiction over the country's air policy.

One of Howe's first appointments was to promote his "Boy Wonder" Crawford Gordon, in late 1944, from an assistant coordinator of production to the more senior position of director general of Industrial Reconversion. Both Munitions and Supply and Reconstruction and Supply were excellent training grounds for Gordon, now barely 30. Not only was he able to get a rare look deep inside Canadian industry, but he was also able to see first-hand how shortages and reliance on offshore sources of supply could bring assembly lines to a halt. In addition, he got a look at the problems companies had in converting from wartime back to peacetime production.

Ottawa, and indeed the whole country, was a much different place in 1945 than it had been in the dark early war days of five years before. Throughout 1945, and especially after VJ day in August, C.D. Howe found himself saying goodbye to his dollar-a-year men almost daily as they returned to their own companies. In December, Crawford Gordon joined the exodus when he tendered his resignation as director general of the Industrial Reconversion branch. He was eager to return to his pre-war company, Canadian General Electric, and the impending (or so he thought) promotion to President.

I must tender my resignation, he wrote to Howe on December 12, as director general of the Industrial Reconversion branch, in order to return to my company. I would like to take this opportunity of telling you how much I have valued the experience of working under you over this past four years in the various posts I have held … It has been a great privilege.[46]

Howe replied: Each day I seem to be faced with the unpleasant task of saying goodbye to one or other of the men who have been associated with me during the past six years. I can appreciate your desire to return to your company, but at the same time, I am extremely sorry to lose your services. While we did not see as much of each other during the early years of the war as we have in recent months, I know how much you have had to do with the success of our production program in the Ontario area. I wish you to know how much I appreciate the assistance and loyalty you have given me at all times. You have been a tower of strength to me.…[47]

Although no member of the dollar-a-year club wore the C.D. Howe badge with greater pride, Gordon knew any success he would have in a post war world would be because of him and him alone — not because he was a "Howe Boy".

Gordon's war work did not go unrewarded. In the Dominion Day awards of July 1, 1946, in which outstanding Canadian civilians are recognized, Gordon received an Order of the British Empire (OBE). Of the 196 awarded that day, only 13 went to Howe's Boys. At 31, Crawford Gordon was the youngest.

He wouldn't have guessed it at the time, but in five short years, Gordon would return to Ottawa to work again with Howe, this time in his Department of Defence Production (DDP). The mentor/Boy Wonder, Howe/Gordon combination would click once more.

Chapter Three

POST-WAR: RETURN TO PRIVATE BUSINESS (1946-51)

BACK TO CANADIAN GENERAL ELECTRIC

*T*he war had been good to Canadian companies and Canadian General Electric was no exception. Its net income had averaged $2.3 million and excess profit taxes had ballooned to $4.5 million during the same period. When Gordon returned to the scene in January 1946, the company was well into peacetime conversion, both in expansion and rehabilitation of their existing facilities. A new building was being constructed in Peterborough for small motors, a new small-appliance plant was being built in Barrie, Ontario and an additional building was added to the company's Toronto Davenport works plant. Gordon's old boss, Hal Turner, had been made vice president in 1942 and then president in 1946.

Coming out of Munitions and Supply as one of Howe's Boys proved to be the greatest work experience to date in the life of the 31-year-old Crawford Gordon; and with an OBE to boot! The years with Howe had hardened his determination that if he put his mind to it, literally anything was possible. What remained to be seen, however, was just how content this young man in a hurry would be returning to the mundane job in the auditing department at Canadian General Electric. When Gordon arrived back on the scene, he was given the vague title of assistant to the president. Mary and the family were on the move once again. Now there were five of them, Diana having been born in Toronto on March 4, 1944. "Hurry up and have this child," Gordon would tell Mary just before the birth, "I'm missing a hockey game!"[1]

* * * *

In Malton, the Victory Aircraft Company was winding down operations at a fierce rate, laying off 500 wartime employees per week. The company had barely 1,000 people left from a wartime high of 10,000. Since his visit and meeting with Howe in 1943, Sir Roy Dobson had kept in touch with both Howe and his "young man in Canada," Fred Smye. Dobson "valued and asked for C.D.'s advice often"[2] over the two years since they'd met and for Howe, Dobson was clearly someone with whom he could do business.

"[Howe] was irritable and impatient with the cautious easy way of Canadians," writes Peter C. Newman. "He felt that they hung back, had little zest, demanded assurance of a big return on their money before they'd start anything. The boys with the risk money … *theirs* was the language he understood."[3]

In October 1945 Dobson returned to Canada in hopes of closing the deal to take over Victory Aircraft, which at the time, consisted of over one million square feet of physical plant including three large assembly bays. Dobson felt he could convince his employer, now called the Hawker-Siddeley Group of companies, to take over one assembly bay and perhaps some administration space. After all, who would want to get into the aviation business at a time when everyone was getting out of it? Howe, on the other hand, saw it as an opportunity to unload that deserted, unused industrial space and he was prepared to make the terms more than generous if he had to.

With Fred Smye in tow, Dobson took rooms in the Château Laurier and went off to see the minister alone. "He had in his little black briefcase the plan," recalls Smye, "and when he returned to the room he threw his briefcase on the bed and said: 'Well Freddie, we've taken the whole bloody thing!'"[4] And the terms had indeed been generous. The contract between Howe and Dobson called for taking over the Victory plant on a sort of "rent to purchase" basis; that is to say, Dobson would get the entire operation for $2.5 million, but wouldn't have to pay the money up front, just be covered for it. And he wouldn't have to pay any rent until this new company started making money. In return for his generosity, Howe demanded a number of conditions:

- The new company would be Canadian.

- The company would get into design and development, not just assembly under licence.

- The Hawker-Siddeley parent would train Canadians in up-to-date design, development and research.

- The company's president would always be Canadian.

> *For a period, Dobson announced to the press soon after, the Canadian company will be a design, research and development affair with no aircraft being produced. We are putting into Canada a team of designers. I do not expect there is much we shall need to get from here (England) except technical guidance. We have not gone into Canada as a moneymaking organization; we have gone in to spread development of the science of aeronautics and to give Canada a basic industry which, in our opinion, she badly needs. Canada will become the aircraft production centre of the British Empire within ten years.*[5]

"The whole plan," echoed C.D. Howe the following month "is very satisfying from the standpoint of Canada."[6] Dobson's first order of business was to hire Fred Smye as the new company's first employee and put him on the payroll in his factory with no contracts and no money; but at least there was a deal. "What are you going to do with the place?" asked a shell-shocked Smye on being hired. "I don't know Freddie," replied Dobson, "but we'll do something, we'll get along all right...."[7] They would indeed.

The deal with Howe was signed in November and on December 2, 1945, A.V. Roe Canada came into existence. The china shop was waiting for its bull.

* * * *

Crawford Gordon was languishing as Hal Turner's assistant at the Canadian General Electric head office on King Street in Toronto. The return to the private sector had not been easy for the young man in a hurry that autumn of 1947. Memories of Ottawa and the war were still fresh in his mind. Working with Howe had been exciting, dynamic, a far cry from the dull paperwork and number crunching in which he was now involved. Gordon had great respect for Turner but being second in command was not what he saw for himself. Even the $125 per month salary — good money in those days for a man in his early thirties — was not enough. Gordon was not a happy man.

One day, more to make a point than anything else, Gordon waltzed into Turner's office and said:

"Mr. Turner, I respectfully ask for a reduction in salary." This, of course, caught the president's attention.
"What do you mean you want a reduction in salary?" was the reply.
"Well, I don't think the responsibility you're giving me warrants the money you're paying me."
"Well, what is it exactly you want Crawford?" asked Turner.
"I want to be the president of the company!" was the response.
Turner replied, "You go back to your office and keep your $125 a month and that will keep the wolves from the door and we'll see what happens."[8]

What happened was that just a week later, Turner was asked to lunch with long-time friend Major James Hahn, known affectionately in the business community as Major Hahn from his military service in the First World War. The 45-year-old Hahn was a multifaceted person. An American-born industrialist and entrepreneur, he was also a big-game hunter, a Canadian Army Intelligence veteran, a lawyer and a member of the old boys' network. He was also a visionary with big plans.[9]

In 1923 at the age of 32, Hahn had become head of the DeForest Radio Corporation and in the next ten years, his company produced radios and expanded into other domestic appliances. In 1934 he sold his interest in the company to his main competitor, the Rogers company.

Hahn's personal hobby was a passion for firearms and during a visit to Great Britain in 1936, he witnessed a secret demonstration of a new, Czechoslovakian-developed automatic weapon known as the Bren Gun. This light machine-gun weighed just 21 pounds and fired at the rate of 450 rounds per minute. Easy to assemble, the gun was air cooled and gas operated and was destined to become the standard automatic weapon in the allied arsenal in the Second World War.

Even though it was 1936 and the war was still three years away, and even though Canada was still years from developing any rearmament programs, Major Hahn secured the licence to manufacture the Bren Gun in Canada from the British. All he needed was an order to produce the gun and a factory to produce it in. He would soon receive both.

JOHN INGLIS CORPORATION AND ENGLISH ELECTRIC COMPANY

For 55 years the John Inglis Corporation had operated within sight of downtown Toronto. Its founder, John Inglis, was a metalworker, a skilled pattern maker and a travelling craftsman who had begun his craft in Guelph in 1859. Originally the firm served rural customers including country millers and village shops across Wellington County, specializing in steam engines and boilers, and later produced a number of metal products including chains, window grates, manhole covers, iron plates, replacement parts and doors and covers for forging equipment.

In 1881 the company moved from Guelph to Toronto (a city with a rapidly growing manufacturing sector) to a group of buildings located along Strachan Avenue in Toronto's west end, neighbours of the Massey Manufacturing Company which produced farm equipment. With John's death in 1899, the company was taken over by his oldest son William. Inglis did well in the First World War and in the 1920s, but profits began to slide in the 1930s. By 1936 the plant was in receivership and was reduced to a maintenance staff of just three from a wartime peak of 17,000 workers.

It was on his return from Britain and the Bren Gun demonstration that Major Hahn learned of the deserted Inglis site and quietly purchased it in November of 1936. The following year, British officials decided that the Bren Gun could be produced in Canada, and Hahn convinced them that he had the factory and could recruit the appropriate work force to make it happen. In April, the Inglis company began producing Bren Guns. The contract to produce 7,000 Bren Guns for Canada was not without controversy, both over how Hahn got the contract in the first place and how high the allowable profit on each copy should be. Parliamentary investigations were carried out, nothing really out of the ordinary was uncovered, and Hahn's Strachan Avenue plant went on to turn out 186,000 Bren Guns for the war effort. Even today the Inglis company, or what's left of it, is known as the "Bren Gun Factory."[10]

* * * *

Hal Turner and James Hahn hadn't seen each other much since the war, so their lunch meeting in the fall of 1947 gave both men a chance to catch up. Hahn went on to tell Turner that Inglis seemed to be faring pretty well in peacetime and had gotten in a number of licencing agreements with other companies to produce a number of domestic products as a way of rebuilding in new directions the company's manufacturing. The former Ordinance Division that had built Bren Guns, for instance, was now called the Consumer Products Division to better reflect post-war manufacturing in Canada. And recently Hahn had bought control of a British company, the English Electric Company in St. Catharines because he wanted to get involved in hydroelectric work. And with the purchase of the company came the licencing agreements to build transformers, switch gears and motors.[11]

It was at this point that Turner mentioned how tired his friend looked. "Dad wanted very much to retire after the war," recalls his son David.

> *He loved hunting and fishing and was worn out from the war. Not only had he run Inglis during the war, C. D. Howe*

*had him working as vice-president of Victory Aircraft in Mal-
ton and he was director general of the Army Technical Devel-
opment Corps. On the personal side, he was president of the
Toronto Symphony, commodore of his yacht club and got the
United Appeal [Red Feather Campaign] started in Toronto.
My brother and I were too young at the time to think of ever
taking over the business, so my father was on the lookout for
a good 'number-two' man. Dad knew full well who Crawford
Gordon was and knew he was number-two man to Hal
Turner.*[12]

During the lunch Hahn told Turner he wanted to talk to Gordon
about running his newly acquired English Electric operation in
St. Catharines. Turner wasn't going to step down from president of
CGE for some time and didn't want to stand in the way of Gordon's
ambitions.

"What do you want for him?" asked Hahn.
"I'll take that cigar you have in your coat, Major," was the reply.
When Hahn came home to dinner that night, he was obviously very
pleased.
"Why are you so happy, Dad?' asked one of his sons.
"Well I just got Crawford Gordon as my number-two man and I got
him for a cigar!"[13]

* * * *

At Malton, Sir Roy Dobson's newly formed A. V. Roe Company was
looking for things, any things, to do. The previous April had seen the
three-hundredth Lancaster bomber roll off the line and, although
lay-offs were occurring almost daily, the company learned they
would soon be producing a couple of Lancaster hybrids: the Lincoln
and the York bombers. That was fine, thought Dobson, but if his
company was really going to take off in Canada, it needed a solid
contract to produce aircraft — and someone to buy them. The only
two organizations in the country at the time in the position to do
that were Trans Canada Airlines (TCA) and the Royal Canadian Air
Force (RCAF). Dobson went to see Trans Canada Airlines first.

In England Dobson had heard rumours that TCA were actively looking for an intercity replacement for the DC-3 and had hopes that the aircraft would be designed and built in Canada. "I understand from some of the Canadian government people here," he wrote to H. J. Symington, the president of TCA, "that there is a possibility of the equipment you have ordered not coming up to delivery schedule and I was wondering, in this case, whether we should be in a position to help you."[14]

Dobson's Hawker-Siddeley Group had been looking into developing a series of commercial aircraft based on their famous Lancaster, planes like the Lancastrian, the York and the Tudor.

"I am coming over to Canada in about a week's time," he added, "and I should very much like to meet you whilst I am there in order to discuss our Tudors." When Dobson arrived in Canada and met Symington, he found him lukewarm on the idea of the Tudor, but much to the chagrin of TCA's president, C.D. Howe, the minister in charge of TCA, was just the opposite. Howe had already gone on record as saying that Dobson's new company would likely, "manufacture large passenger transport planes after the war with the view to meeting competition for world airline traffic."[15] Coming from Symington's boss, it seemed like a done deal. So Dobson cabled the Victory Aircraft plant to come up with a scheme of "working the remaining parts of the Lancasters and Lincolns still there and make them into a Tudor."[16] A.V. Roe did actually secure a contract to convert five Lincolns into Tudors but the contract was cancelled after six months for a much more ambitious project known as the Avro Jetliner.

Next came the RCAF, which was headed at the end of the war by Air Marshall Robert Leckie, a long-time proponent of an independent air force for Canada. And beyond that, he also believed that any future aircraft for the RCAF would be designed and built in Canada, or "home built" as Leckie liked to call it. In 1945 Leckie's RCAF was the third largest air force in the world, in terms of men and equipment. But as had been the case after the First World War the military would quickly demilitarize, leaving the air force with more than enough aircraft for years to come. Leckie told Dobson that if the RCAF was going to buy any new equipment, it would probably be a purely military plane, possibly a trainer, something small and palatable.

Dobson commented years later, "That's not the way Canada is going to grow."[17]

> *On Friday November 3, 1945, Victory Aircraft Ltd. closed its doors for the last time. Supervisors instructed some 150 or so workers to stay close to the phone over the weekend but by the following Monday, only two people showed up for work. One of them was Fred Smye, now working for Roy Dobson. By the end of the week 136 people were at work and by mid-January, there were 350 at the plant. Most of the design offices were deserted save for a couple of engineers sketching away the time on blueprint paper, designing additions to their homes and cottages. The assembly bays were deserted with hundreds of pieces of Lancasters, Lincolns and Yorks stacked up against the wall or hanging from the ceiling like meat in a butcher shop. Outside on the tarmac, finished Lancasters, their wings clipped, hid under the snow.[18]*

Sir Roy Dobson must have felt like a lonely man that winter of 1945-46. From a business point of view, he had done everything he was not supposed to do — getting into the aircraft business when everyone else was getting out. On the one hand, he had what looked like a sweet deal with Howe, albeit riding on a handshake and some scribble on the back of a cigarette package. But he had no takers from the country's two obvious buyers of aircraft, and he certainly had found no interest for Hawker-Siddeley's current project, the Tudor. And the plant he had just bought was all but closed up.

In England, his world was not much brighter. His own Hawker-Siddeley board, with the exception of a few of his pals, had taken a dim view of his venture and were not totally sold on the idea. With assets exceeding $146 million, after a wartime production effort of $2,233 million, and with $42 million in cash on hand, the board was not going to jeopardize any of their holdings, and certainly not on Dobson's venture in Canada with a company with no contracts on the books when such companies were a dime a dozen.

Despite C. D. Howe continuing to preach that "prospects for aircraft production in Canada were encouraging,"[19] he was worried about his British friend. When he heard about the lukewarm reception Dobson had had from Leckie and Symington, Howe decided to give Dobson a chance to get out of the deal during a visit to Ottawa.

"Well, Roy, I suppose you're here because you want out?" asked the minister.
"No," Dobson replied, "I don't want out."
"Well, you've got more guts than brains," was Howe's parting comment.[20]

"With the exception of the Arrow program," recalls Fred Smye, "it was probably our lowest point as a company. Everyone thought Dobson was just plain crazy."[21]

Everyone, that is, except Dobson himself.

*   *   *   *

Crawford Gordon reported for work as president of the English Electric Company in St. Catharines in December of 1947. In addition to that title, Major Hahn made him his "number two" at the John Inglis Company, as executive vice-president. "English Electric was struggling after the war," recalls David Hahn. "And when Dad bought the company, he put Crawford over there to see what was going on and to put it back on its feet."[22]

The English Electric Company in St. Catharines had begun its corporate life in 1908 as the Canadian Crocker Wheeler Corporation, employing close to 200 people producing transformers and electrical parts. In 1922 the company was bought by the English Electric Company of Great Britain and continued in the electrical business producing dynamos, transformers and generators until purchased by Major Hahn's John Inglis company in early 1947. During the war, English Electric had been a hallmark company, and in those days, the factories were built right in the middle of residential areas — the more smoke, the more employment. The company was really an integral part of the St. Catharines community. Old-timers recall that you could set your watch by the company's whistle, five minutes to seven (morning shift), five to noon (lunch) and five to five (end of day.)

Crawford Gordon and his family moved into an apartment on Yates Street in St. Catharines, with a view of the Welland Canal. Diana and Cynthia went to public school and son Crawford attended the local private school, Ridley College (any school, but Appleby!). The children would see their father a lot in those days — one of the last times they would be so fortunate.

As for Mary, the marriage to Crawford, the three children and numerous moves in recent years brought little, if any, complaining. Her life was with her husband and her happiness was with her family. It's all she ever wanted. It's all she ever would want. Nothing more.

As pleased as Major Hahn was to secure the services of Crawford Gordon as his "number two," not everyone in St. Catharines looked forward to his arrival. "St. Catharines was a close community in those days," recalls former journalist Lou Cahill. "There was no lack of leadership here. We had people like Harry Carmichael (for whom Gordon had worked during the war) as vice-president of the TD bank and head of Argus; we had Dr. H. G. Fox, a top corporate lawyer and president of Lightening Fasteners. This was a heavyweight community and I think Gordon was considered a true outsider." That, and the fact that he beat out the popular Hector C. Blenkhorn for the presidency of the company.[23]

Hector Blenkhorn, "Blinkey" to his friends, was vice-president and general manager of the company when Gordon showed up. An MIT grad, like C.D. Howe, Blenkhorn had come from Bell Telephone in 1935 and guided the company through the war years — the company's best years, many thought — when both morale and productivity were at their peak. When Gordon arrived, the predictable happened. "The big joke at English at the time," recalls Jim Gilmore, a company historian "was people taking bets on when Crawford Gordon would march down the hall to fire Blenkhorn. As it turns out, he didn't have to. Blenkhorn didn't like, or get along with, Gordon so he left on his own in early 1948."[24] It might have happened anyway, since Major Hahn felt that "Blenkhorn wasn't really up to the job."[25] That was the reason he'd hired Crawford Gordon in the first place.

To the people at English and to the city of St. Catharines in general, Gordon personified a "new" type of manager — distant, aggressive and decisive. Despite the fact that his family settled into the city, Gordon was rarely home, spending several days a week up the highway at the Inglis plant in Toronto. Even young Crawford didn't get a chance to mix in the local social scene because his father had enrolled him at the prestigious Ridley College, a school hardly affordable to most locals.

Gordon seemed different in other ways as well. "One time some couples from St. Catharines were on a cruise," recalls a company insider, "and someone said, 'You folks'll be glad to know there's another couple on the cruise as well: Crawford Gordon and his wife. I'll arrange for them to be at your table tonight for dinner.' And when Mr. and Mrs. Gordon arrived for dinner, Mrs. Gordon wasn't *the* Mrs. Gordon."

And was Major Hahn pleased with his decision to bring in Crawford Gordon? "Dad never second-guessed his decision to hire Gordon for a moment," recalls his son David. "The only time he ever felt disappointed was one time Gordon bought an expensive company car for himself and didn't tell Dad. Dad wouldn't have cared but he felt he should have been consulted and felt it was done behind his back. But any regrets? No. None."[26]

* * * *

The company that would one day design and build the sophisticated Avro Arrow aircraft got its start making plastic hairbrushes and tractor parts. "When we came back," recalls Bob Johnson of those first days, "they broke the 300 or so of us up into two groups: one worked for War Assets [the government purchasing agency] for $1 per hour and the other group were involved in engineering, planning and tooling."[27] They did just about everything: making forms for plastic hairbrushes, making truck fenders, designing and testing oil burners, manufacturing parts for tractors. Then, through War Assets, came the contracts to overhaul and repair surplus aircraft. Sea Furys, Harvards, DC-3s, Dakotas, Mitchels, Hudsons and Lancasters began arriving from all over the country to have their gas tanks emptied, their wings taken off and their engines removed. And then the RCAF asked the company to convert Lancasters to Lancastrians for reconnaissance work.

For this early work, A.V. Roe received payment through C.D. Howe's new Department of Reconstruction and Supply. They were paid retroactively for the previous month's work. No work, no payment. From its first day of operation, the company operated on a "cost-plus" basis, that is, the cost to do the job plus a 5 per cent profit. Since Dobson had the use of the property on a sort of rent-to-purchase basis, it made sense for the government to give as much work as possible to A.V. Roe in order to recover its investment in the shortest possible time. In fact, they received so many contracts that A.V. Roe was able to pay off the $2.5 million purchase price by August 1948.

While his men toiled away making hairbrushes and truck parts, Dobson turned his attention to finding his "number one." He wanted someone who was clearly "an aircraft man" like himself, someone well respected in the industry and, in keeping with his agreement with Howe, someone Canadian. He found him in a quiet, unassuming man with a grey toothbrush moustache — Walter Deischer. Deischer had been general manager of Fleet Aircraft in Fort Erie, Ontario during the war and had surpassed a number of US production schedules on wartime aircraft. Known for his twice-a-day walks through the Fleet plant, and delegating total authority to his department heads, critics would say he lacked leadership, was a daydreamer of sorts and could get consumed with the most minor of details. "I walked out of his office lots of times believing he was crazy," one of his staff would say later. "He'd sit there for an hour and discuss things and you'd go away believing he'd made a firm decision. Then, 15 minutes later, he'd change his mind."[28]

Walter Deischer was born in Virginia and had immigrated to Canada in 1913 at the age of 24. Before the Second World War, his experience was largely in the auto industry, having raced cars in the 1930s. But he had always been keen on flying, and liked to display his pilot's card signed by Orville Wright. To almost everyone he met, he was a nice little man, yet "masking a terrible fear he had about meeting people."[29] "He'd sit behind that desk of his," recalls former aviation writer Jim Hornick, "and he'd sign things and somebody would wind him up and he'd walk to the window."[30] But, despite what people said, Roy Dobson had himself a "number one."

* * * *

In St. Catharines, being president of the English Electric Company didn't pose any difficult challenges for Crawford Gordon, but at least he could say he was the boss. But most of the action, and most of Gordon's time, was occupied with the activities at the Inglis parent plant in Toronto.

Management, under Major Hahn's leadership, had been vigorously exploring peacetime production possibilities at Inglis as early as 1942 and created a consumer goods division, a name change that symbolized post-war manufacturing in Canada. Since the turn of the century, Inglis products had pumped away in the heart of most Canadian ships, breweries, steel mill, refineries, sewage plants, mines and skating rinks. If they could do that for Canadian industry, surely they could do that for Canadian homes as well.[31]

Half of Gordon's time was spent in his office in St. Catharines and the other, more exciting half of his time, was spent at the John Inglis plant on Strachan Avenue in Toronto. Gordon's experience in setting up wartime production under C. D. Howe would prove to be equally valuable in setting up peacetime production of consumer goods. This fact was not lost on the Major. And then the unexpected happened.

Major Hahn, Gordon's boss and CEO of the John Inglis Corporation, was still anxious to retire and decided to sell his controlling interests in both companies back to the English Electric Company of Great Britain which he'd bought out just four years before. Out of his respect for Gordon, he advised him of the move in advance and indicated that, because of the sale, his future might be a little "clouded."[32]

"How much time do I have?" asked Gordon.

"I expect," replied Hahn, "that the deal will be complete by January 1951."

When Gordon got off the phone, he sat for a moment in the quiet of his office and thought about his options. He couldn't go back to CGE because Turner was still the president. Both the companies in which he was currently senior executive were about to be sold to the Brits and that could mean anything. He had heard that because of Cold War pressures, Canada was about to get into the defence production business once again, although obviously not on the scale of the Second World War. But the man scheduled to run the whole operation was his mentor C. D. Howe. Perhaps this is what he was looking for.

"Hello," he would ask the switchboard of the English Electric Company in St. Catharines, "Get me Ottawa on the line. I'd like to talk to C. D. Howe."

It was late December 1950.

Chapter Four

RETURN TO OTTAWA: DEPARTMENT OF DEFENCE PRODUCTION AND AVRO'S FIRST PROJECTS (1951)

THE AVRO JETLINER

*A*t Malton, Roy Dobson now had a company employing 300, a couple of contracts for the overhaul of war surplus aircraft and a man in charge — company president Walter Deischer. But what he really wanted were good, solid aircraft design and development contracts that would provide the foundation that his new company needed to give it a secure future. The contracts came from the two unlikeliest of sources, the same two organizations Dobson had gone to hat in hand but a few months before: Trans Canada Airlines and the Royal Canadian Air Force. One project involved a pure jet transport aircraft and the other a front-line fighter for the air force. It now seemed that Dobson's "little empire in Canada" might finally take off.

"The birth of the C-102 Avro Jetliner," writes Jim Floyd, the plane's designer, "was almost coincidental with the birth of the company.[1] On a visit to Canada in mid-1945, Sir Roy Dobson had a discussion over drinks with Jim Bain,[2] then chief engineer with Trans Canada Airlines, about the possibility of his new Canadian company building a medium-range jet transport for TCA. Dobbie was keen on getting in on the ground floor to exploit the new jet engine technology, developed in the latter part of the Second World War and Jim Bain became enamoured with the idea of TCA being the first airline to operate a jet transport.

"At that time I was Davie's chief project engineer at the Avro factory in Yorkshire. Among other things, we had been looking at turbo transport possibilities, for both turboprop and pure jet engines."

Specifications and sketches for this new transport aircraft were drafted including both turboprop and pure jet versions. Originally favored was a safe, 36-seat turboprop aircraft but TCA's Jim Bain was adamant that any transport aircraft destined for his company must be powered by straight jet engines. As this debate was going on A. V. Roe Canada had been formed in Malton with Walter Deischer as president and Fred Smye his second in command.

Jim Floyd continues: "One day (Dobson's top technical man Stu Davies) walked into my office and out of the blue asked, 'How would you like to go to Canada … and continue work on the jet transport over there?' I was on my way in a few days, landing in Malton in a snowstorm in late January 1946."

When Floyd arrived, the plant was virtually empty save for a small nucleus of engineers, hold-overs from Victory Aircraft, who had been persuaded to stay on.

"In April 1946," continues Floyd, "a couple of former Victory Aircraft engineers accompanied me to TCA engineering headquarters in Winnipeg to firm up the jet transport specification and preliminary design for the aircraft now earmarked as the Avro C-102. H. J. Symington, president of TCA, immediately followed up with a letter of intent to Deischer saying that TCA would be in the market for 30 of these aircraft if the agreed specification was met.

"We returned to Toronto and design work on the C-102 commenced immediately, the engineering team building up to approximately 100 people."

Design work on the jet transport continued at a hectic pace until word was received from Rolls Royce in the United Kingdom that the two engines they had promised for the plane — AJ-65s — had run into difficulty and they were possibly years away from supplying a certified civil version for use. Offered instead was a Derwent engine with half the thrust of the AJ-65. This meant Floyd's team would have to design an aircraft to accommodate four instead of two engines. The Derwent fuel consumption was also higher, resulting in a weight increase to the aircraft and other problems. There were some advantages, however. Floyd's team had a well-proven engine, four-engine reliability, better take-off capabilities in hot and high conditions and other considerations.

Floyd's team pushed ahead with the project and modified the design so that the aircraft would still meet the TCA requirements. In the meantime, however, there had been some contractual disagreements between the company, the airline and the Canadian government centring around the production cost of the aircraft. A. V. Roe felt it could not give a firm price until the airline made up its mind about the number of aircraft it wanted and the airline was not prepared to reach a decision on numbers until the aircraft had flown, with a firm price established.

"We returned to TCA with the modified four-engine design in October 1947," continues Floyd, "and TCA issued a report on its reaction in February 1948 from which it became obvious that TCA management had had second thoughts about going out on a limb as the first airline to operate a straight jet transport.

"TCA engineers informed us that due mainly to the disappointingly slow development of the Instrument Landing Systems (ILS) at Canadian airports, their fuel allowances would have to be drastically increased. They also broke the news that they had had second thoughts on many other requirements as set out in the previously agreed specification. That must have been the understatement of 1948!"

Whatever the reason, TCA's participation and interest in the C-102, now called the Avro Jetliner, was over, more than ten months before the aircraft's first flight. Participation did not cease politically, however, and under government pressure TCA was constantly asked to comment on the progress of flight-testing and development of the Jetliner.

"I personally feel this was a ridiculous imposition on an airline which had already expressed its disinterest in the project," recalls Floyd, "and it resulted in the inevitable defensive criticisms which such a situation is sure to generate."

The first prototype flew first on August 10, 1949, just 25 months after the design of the Derwent-engined version had started and just 13 days after Britain's de Havilland Comet, the world's first jet transport, took to the air. The flight program went unbelievably well. On inter-city flights all over the US and Canada the Jetliner cut flight times in half. The many US airline executives carried on these flights were, without exception, enthusiastic about the aircraft.

On one memorable flight from Toronto to New York City, the Jetliner became the first jet in the world to carry airmail. The next day the New York press carried pictures of the jetliner flying over the city, with the comment: "This should give our nation a good healthful kick in its placidity. The fact that our massive but underpopulated good neighbor to the north has a mechanical product that licks anything of ours is just what the doctor ordered for our overdeveloped ego. The Canadian plane's feat accelerates a process already begun in this nation — a realization that Uncle Sam has no monopoly on genius."[3]

Yet as well as an aircraft performs, it's no good to anyone, least of all to those that designed and built it, unless it can be sold.

THE CF-100

"I was the leader of a special team of RCAF officers," recalls former Air Marshal Wilf Curtis, "who visited aircraft factories in the UK and US looking for an aircraft. We couldn't find one ... it became obvious that if our air force was to have the kind of aircraft our planners said it needed, we would have to design it ourselves. That is precisely how the CF-100 was born."[4]

In 1942 Curtis had performed what for him was a strange and frustrating duty. The Japanese were in the Aleutian Islands ready at any moment to sweep down Canada's west coast, and the RCAF had no aircraft to stop them. Curtis had to appear before an aircraft allotment conference and plead with Allies for aircraft which had been built in Canada but were destined for other countries and other air forces. His pleas fell on deaf ears. The Hurricane fighters, built at Fort William Ontario, went to the Soviet Union anyway.

"Maybe they needed the planes more than we did," he would reflect later. "I don't know. But I do know that we needed them very badly. And I realized right then, walking out of that room and feeling every inch a failure, that until we didn't have to tip our hats to anyone to get aircraft when we needed them, we'd never have the air force a first rate nation really deserves."[5]

Due in part to Air Marshall Robert Leckie who always felt Canada should have aircraft that were "home built," and in part to Curtis' wartime experience, the RCAF issued their very first specification for an aircraft even before the war was over. In January 1945 specification Air-7-1 was released and tentatively called for the design and production of a single-engine, single-seat jet aircraft.

At A.V. Roe, Fred Smye got hold of the air specifications and passed them along to some of his engineers at Malton to see what they could come up with. The company was still a small operation involved in the aircraft overhaul projects from War Assets and the RCAF; Jim Floyd, Avro's chief project engineer, was engaged in the jet transport project; and a third group was informally organized to respond to the RCAF requirement.

The original specifications were changed after the war to better reflect the realities of the Cold War. With our former Soviet ally capable of launching a bombing raid over the polar ice cap, Canada would need more than a few squadrons of Second World War surplus aircraft to stop it.

"The role of the CF-100," writes Jim Floyd, "was to provide the RCAF with a truly all-weather day and night fighter with long range and very high speed at high altitude. It had to be equipped with sophisticated radar and weaponry and had to be able to operate from minimum service runway facilities. It may not be appreciated decades later what a tall order this was at that time when successful jet fighters could still be counted on the fingers of one hand. The aircraft carried about the same fuel load as a Second World War bomber and the armament in the later versions was equal in fire power to that of a naval cruiser."[6]

The original contract between the government of Canada and A.V. Roe called for the production of 718 complete aircraft and 738 spare engines not including ten pre-production prototype aircraft. The 718 aircraft were expected to cost $360,000 per plane plus $60,000 for each of the planes' two engines, for a total cost of $480,000. This price included the company's cost plus 5 per cent rule. Total cost to the Canadian government: $544,500,000.

The aircraft first flew in January 1950, and despite the loss of one of the prototypes that killed the pilot and the observer, the aircraft was finally delivered to the RCAF in a formal ceremony at Malton on October 18, 1951. It was now known as the CF-100 Canuck. "This aircraft," beamed C.D. Howe, present at the ceremony and whose Department of Reconstruction and Supply had put up the money for the plane, "is a notable Canadian achievement, marking as it does a new milestone in Canada's industrial process ... It is a triumph of skill and ingenuity. I am satisfied that Canada will lead all countries in the production of this type of aircraft."[7]

"Five years is a short time for any country to produce from the planning stage to production a modern fighter aircraft," echoed Air Marshall Wilf Curtis, also present for the ceremony. "A. V. Roe can be justly proud of its achievements."[8] Air Vice Marshall McGill summed up the feelings of many: "I don't believe the public at large has any appreciation of the difficulty in producing an aircraft..."[9] It wouldn't be long before they would find out. In less than a week the air force returned the aircraft to the company. Flight Lieutenant Joe Schultz was the RCAF pilot who returned that CF-100 to the tarmac at Malton. "When I landed the aircraft at Malton, it was an interesting sight: rivets and things were hanging on to the bottom of the wings through the cracks. The engine [compartments] had cracked because the wings had flexed [it was] bent 30 degrees. Quite a mess."[10]

Fred Smye panicked, and without telling Roy Dobson, invited some of Dobson's key stress people to go over the aircraft and see if it could be fixed.

"Burn it," was the recommendation.
"Burn what?" asked Smye not sure of what they meant.

"Burn the plane, every bloody part of it. It's understressed. We haven't got time to build a new one so go to Howe and tell him you can build Northrop Scorpions under licence."[11]

Gathering what was left of his composure, Smye thanked the men and ignored their recommendation. There must be another way, he thought. But what to do about a solution if one, in fact, existed.

THE ENGINES

Even though A. V. Roe was an aircraft company and was tentatively in the business to produce a jet transport for passenger travel and a jet fighter for the RCAF, the company's first success stories were, interestingly enough, in jet engines.

In April 1946, Sir Roy, as he now liked to be called since receiving a knighthood for his efforts with the Lancaster bomber, was once again in Canada and dining with his friend C.D. Howe in Ottawa. Howe was bemoaning the fact that after three years of work and promising results, Canada might have to get out of the jet engine business. Dobson's eyes widened as they always did when caught off guard. He had been well aware of his own country's efforts to design and build a workable gas turbine engine, largely through Frank Whittle and his Power Jets company, but he had no idea that Canada had been active in this field as well.

From as far back as 1943, the government, through the National Research Council and later a Crown corporation called Turbo Research in Leaside, Ontario, had been doing research work on gas turbine engines. Knowing that Canada's focus after the war would be on air defence, the RCAF had issued an operational requirement for a fighter which would eventually become the CF-100 and for an engine as well.

"We figured," recalls former Air Vice Marshall John Easton, "that a 5,000 lbs thrust axial flow engine would do it. We wanted an axial engine over the conventional centrifugal engine because it had greater potential, was a smoother engine and easier to keep pressure under control."[12]

Told to develop an engine that would basically fit a 32-inch hole, the engineers at Turbo Research, led by a brilliant engineer named Winnett Boyd, had laid down a design by Christmas 1945 that would eventually become the famous Orenda. Howe had been told that to keep Turbo Research in operation for the normal five-year engine-development period, it would cost the Canadian taxpayers $8 million, and he had been advised by his staff to try and find a buyer.

"So there really isn't anybody," Howe lamented to Dobson over dinner that spring evening in Ottawa, "who has the guts to take it on."
"I have," said Dobson.
"You!" remarked the minister. "Your plate's full now. Besides what do you know about engines?"
"Not much," was the reply. "But they've always been one of my little hobbies."[13]

Dobson had Turbo Research and its small staff moved from Leaside to the A.V. Roe site in Malton in March 1946.

For some months and years Winnett Boyd, assisted by a competent design and engineering team, continued to work on his engines. The Chinook ran for the first time on St. Patrick's Day 1948 and proved a most capable "teething ring" for the engine they called the "Big One." The Big One, the company's cash crop, was the Orenda. It had its first run on February 10, 1949 and reached its expected thrust of 6,500 lbs. This was the engine that would power the company's other project in the making — the CF-100. Winnett Boyd had filled the 32-inch hole after all. "The future of the entire company," reflected Fred Smye later, "hung on those two little engines."[14]

* * * *

Gordon's phone call to C.D. Howe paid off. In early 1951, Crawford Gordon became a dollar-a-year man for the second time. "Am organizing new defence production department," Howe telegrammed Gordon on February 5, "and most anxious to obtain your services as director of production … suggest you discuss situation with your English [Electric] associates expressing my wish to make your services available to us … sincerely hope you can accept." And eagerly accept he did on March 15.

This new department, writes Bothwell and Kilbourne, "was a miniature version of Munitions and Supply. It processed many of the same functions and many of the statutory powers of its predecessor, but it did not have many occasions to use them. What Howe had escaped in the Second World War — dependence on the Canadian military's orders only — had now come to pass. Between April and December, the new department placed almost $1.5 billion worth of defence orders. Of that, only just over $100 million was for foreign customers. Where Munitions and Supply had been a freewheeling agency largely independent of Canadian requirements, Defence Production was strictly a subordinate purchasing agency for the Canadian Armed Forces.[15]

Basically DDP was made up of three branches: a Materials branch, a General Purchasing branch and a Production branch. Each had its own coordinator reporting directly to Howe. For his production coordinator Howe wanted Crawford Gordon. Barely 38 years old at this time, Gordon found himself responsible for a three-year, $5 billion defence budget covering eight key areas:

- Defence Construction;
- Small Industries;

- Electronics;

- Mechanical Transport;

- Machine Tools;

- Guns and Ammunition;

- Shipbuilding; and

- Aircraft Production.

Gordon made quite an impression on his return to Ottawa. "Gordon is a hard-hitting blunt businessman," wrote *Saturday Night* magazine on his appointment. "He's getting a little thin on top; his face is rugged, but still youthful and full of vigour. He looks no more than his 38 years. Everything about him suggests the phrase: No Fooling!"

"The 38 year old executive," added the *Ottawa Standard*, "is of medium height, quiet spoken, reserved and reticent about his own accomplishments. He has few of the characteristics of a young man in a hurry. He gives the impression of having his feet solidly on the ground. He finds much of his relaxation in a closely knit family circle."[16] *Time* magazine called him "one of the half dozen top manufacturing executives in the country."[17]

Bascially, Gordon's two main jobs in DDP were to obtain from the United States key components needed to manufacture and to establish a Canadian capacity for all the things to be made here. "The last time was an all out effort for war," Gordon would say on his appointment. "This time we're preparing for defence. Last time we had to dislocate everything to produce and we could do it. But this time we're trying to contribute to NATO and to our own defence with a minimum of dislocation. I didn't expect to be back [to Ottawa] so soon. But I'll be here as long as practicable. Of course a lot will depend on Mr. Stalin."[18]

The first priority of the new Defence Production coordinator was to produce aircraft. Only two companies in Canada were in the aircraft production business at the time. Canadair was producing American F86E Sabres under licence at their plant in Montreal at the rate of 20 to 30 per month. The other company was A.V. Roe in Malton and its CF-100 program. Initially the company had been asked to produce five aircraft per month, but with the Korean War imminent, this figure had been upped to 25. Yet not one aircraft had been delivered to the RCAF.

When questioned as to why the CF-100 was not ready and in service with the air force, the company tried to point out that the time taken from original design to delivery was expected to take some 37 months, better than the British average, they said, of 38 months and the American average of 44 months. But if one considers that the company began design after this issue of air spec. Air-7-1 in 1945, its boast of 37 months now became 75 months. If the Korean War had begun in 1953 instead of 1951, the CF-100 might have been ready.

And no one was more aware of this than C.D. Howe and his new Defence Production Coordinator Crawford Gordon.

* * * *

Unsure of how long Gordon would be working at DDP, it was decided that the family would stay in Toronto, with Crawford managing the country's defence production and Mary managing the family's three children. In Ottawa, Gordon threw himself into his role as Defence Production coordinator. But it wasn't all office work, memos or production schedules. He considered one of his roles with the department was to make the country aware of what the Department of Defence Production was and how it was playing a key role in the defence of Canada.

This suited Howe fine since the Minister was never comfortable talking in public about what he did, or making speeches to service clubs and the like. He was more than happy to hand that chore to his man Gordon. In a speech to the business association known as Industrial Canada in July 1951, Gordon talked about the problems of keeping the military rearmed in peacetime:

> *In many ways it is a tougher job than we had at the beginning of the last war. It is more difficult to plan and more dif-*

ficult to execute, and the majority of the stores and munitions are completely new. While we must get into production of the many stores required by the armed service, we do not have any great demand for the end products in many of the fields. In 1939 we could start immediately on volume production of ammunition, explosives, military vehicles and many other items. Short of a full-scale shooting war, volume production of such items can build up awfully quickly, and of course, last time we were producing at peak rates not only to supply our own forces, but to supply Britain and our other allies who were pressed and unable to fill their own needs.[19]

In July he was on the circuit again, this time speaking to the National Defence College, about the problems of defence production for the Korean War.

In my work in the department, I hear a good deal about the production and procurement problems affecting some of our major military programs. The first is that Canada's defence program is strongly influenced by the policies of other countries, particularly the United States. The second is that measures required to carry out the defence program are affected by what is happening in the non-defence or civilian part of the economy. The third is that defence preparations have to be made on the basis of conjectures about the timing of aggression. The fourth is that technical progress in military production is so rapid now that we run the risk of producing arms, which will quickly be outmoded.

We can all hope that the enemy suffers from the same problem.[20]

"Our dollar-a-year men draw no salary from the government," said the *Montreal Standard*, "only modest, civil service scale expenses which allow them little more than a hotel room and three meals a day. And they work hard. Most of them put in five full days a week, often stretching into the evenings, at their Ottawa desks — then fly to their homes in Toronto or Montreal or elsewhere for weekends with their families and a few hours to check the state of their own businesses."[21]

The eighty or so eager young men who made up Howe's DDP were each assigned an eager young woman as support staff, administrative assistant or secretary keen on serving their bosses. Aside from the common clerical functions, they became confidants, protectors of the boss, guardians of the inner office and, in some cases, closer than many family members. Gordon's secretary was a young lady he had brought with him from the John Inglis Corporation, a common practice among company executives in those days. The petite, attractive 25-year-old from Toronto was athletic, had a great sense of humour and a singing voice like Judy Garland's. And she was alone. Her name was Audrey Underwood.

It began with a working lunch, then a drink after dinner, then working late into the night. He was alone (Mary and the family were in Toronto) and she was alone in Ottawa at a time when that city had few places to go, few things to see and do and where the nightclub and social scene were practically non-existent. They began spending more and more time with each other and the lunches involved less and less work and the evenings less and less stenography. There were long talks into the night about his days in Jamaica and the playing fields of Appleby, of her growing up in North Toronto and her fondness for tennis, the theatre and golf, of his mother on the Titanic, of her sister living in sunny California.

They took long walks along the canal in the summer and trips together on the train for a Toronto weekend with their families. Gordon's weekends were family full, of course, and for Audrey, it was tennis at the Carlton Club or the theatre with friends. And it was her friends that started to notice a difference in her, the kind of difference that only friends notice when a young lady has fallen for someone. Lots of people noticed. "There was electricity whenever they were together," recalls a friend of Audrey's. "But sometimes the electricity in getting to a relationship is different than being in a relationship."[22]

For Audrey, the Sunday-night trips to Ottawa with Crawford could never come soon enough. The guy that could "charm the pants off" just about every woman he met had done just that to Audrey, a woman who would stay with him, in one way or another, for the rest of his life. And he with her. On one side was a powerful industrialist, selectively groomed to be what he was, and on the other, was a fun-loving woman, full of life. They ran heart long into each other in the grey, dull post-war Ottawa of 1951. Crawford and Audrey, as unlikely as it was, as unlikely as they were, had fallen in love.

* * * *

At Malton at the A.V. Roe Company, Fred Smye was a troubled man. Working seven days a week, usually 12-hour days, his six-foot frame seemed everywhere, in and out of offices, on the tarmac, in the assembly bays doing all manner of things. Smye was as visible as company president Walter Deischer had become invisible, preferring instead to isolate himself in his office so he wouldn't have to face the problems. And there were problems a plenty.

In the hangar was the Avro Jetliner which they hadn't been able to sell, even to the country's own airline, TCA. Outside on the tarmac were the six CF-100s sitting just where the air force had returned them, loose rivets and all, a few weeks before. In the assembly bays, CF-100 production had come to a complete standstill. At a time when the company should have been furiously hiring to get the plane into production, it was laying off more than 200 employees per week.

Smye would lie awake at night stewing over the Jetliner he couldn't sell, the plane the air force didn't want and his company president who was anything but presidential. "I had 13 loyal people working for me," he would reflect years later, "and every one of them knew we weren't doing well."[25] Late at night the maintenance workers would often find Smye in one of the jet engine test cells. Watching and listening to the engines run gave him some comfort and helped him to sleep.

The relationship between the company, Ottawa and Howe had deteriorated from the wonderful days of 1945. Howe was taking a battering in the House of Commons almost daily over the CF-100.

Typical was this broadside from then Conservative defence critic Douglas Harkness during Question Period:

> *When the CF-100 was first test-flown in January 1950 ... and when the first production orders were given in June 1950, on each occasion there was a great deal of fanfare by the government. The impression was given to everyone in the country that the best long-range fighter in the world would start rolling off the assembly lines and go into service with RCAF squadrons almost immediately. Today the RCAF has none of these fighters. Last October, again with great publicity and fanfare, the CF-100 was turned over to the RCAF. A few weeks later it was taken back to Malton where it was manufactured, and it is still there. The story is that it is undergoing minor changes and so on. Quite apparently, the turning over of this one machine, which was not ready to be turned over, was done for political and publicity purposes. This is not the way our defence efforts should be treated ... It would seem quite apparent that the machine should never have been turned over to the RCAF ... We are not getting these aircraft and engines which we were led to expect ... in fact we were told that our squadrons would be equipped with them now. I do not think that there is any doubt that the government made a bad miscalculation in connection with these aircraft....*[24]

And as Howe's Defence Production chief, Crawford Gordon had gotten into the act as well. Even though he recognized the company was making "steady progress" on the CF-100 and Orenda programs, he felt they had a "very difficult job on their hands." Looking at the situation at A.V. Roe, he thought, "was not unlike the farmer who kept a family cow on which he lavished considerable care and attention. The farmer, oddly enough, kept accounts and his affection for the cow dwindled somewhat when he found that her milk was costing *him* 75 cents a quart."[25]

So when Howe and Gordon got hammered over the CF-100, they, in turn, hammered A.V. Roe. "They were both 'rough as hell' on us over that plane," Fred Smye would say years later. "If we had told Howe how bad things really were with the company and the CF-100 then, he would have scrapped the plane and engine for sure."[26]

But what bothered Howe more than anything at the time was the feeling he had literally gambled millions of dollars on inexperience. He couldn't do much about the plane at this time but he could do something about the company — or at least its president, Walter Deischer.

"Manager of Avro Reported Quitting," said the headline in the *Montreal Gazette* on October 11, 1951, "as a result of internal strife, political interference and government indecision." And, of course, the CF-100.

"Right from the start we had misgivings about Walter," recalls a former company executive. "The man never really knew what he was doing. He'd done a good job at Fleet [Aircraft], but it was a different game at Malton."[27]

One company executive recalls walking into Deischer's office one day with a reporter just when the problems with the CF-100 were starting to surface, and catching him sitting behind his desk casually reading a newspaper. When asked by the reporter how things were going with the Jetliner and the CF-100, Deischer responded: "Well there are a lot of fellows working out there and when you put all that effort in, something's got to come out in the end."[28]

"The job of running A.V. Roe was really too much for poor Walter," adds Fred Smye. "He really knew bugger all about airplanes ... He was from the biplane era, for God's sake. Just how bad he was for us will never be known."[29]

But what to do about a replacement? Dobson had to be careful not to make the same mistake again, especially now. He had to find someone who would put Howe at ease and restore his confidence in the company, someone Howe could trust to get results, someone definitely Canadian, familiar with large-scale production and its problems, and who, in Smye's words "would buy us insurance in the future."

"Well, what about Fred Smye?" asked Dobson.
"If you put Smye in charge," replied Howe, "you'll kill him."
"Well, who do you have in mind?"
"My Crawford Gordon in Defence Production."

Chapter Five

A.V. ROE CANADA
(1951-59)

"FIXING" THE CF-100

*"I*n many ways he was a lot like E.P. Taylor," Fred Smye would say of Crawford Gordon years later, "impatient and impetuous. He was certainly the strongest guy I ever met in my life — a great athlete, a great golfer, full of vitality."[1] John Porter, in his famous work *The Vertical Mosaic*, says that men like Gordon occupied a position in life, "somewhere between influence and power,"[2] but to the workers in the plant at A.V. Roe who can recall Gordon's arrival that autumn of 1951, the feeling was almost unanimous. "He was a big, big man," said one. "He thought big, he acted big, he did things big."[3]

"Gordon's appointment came as a surprise," wrote aviation writer Jim Hornick in *The Globe and Mail*, "both to government and to the rank and file of Avro employees at Malton … He will take charge of the Avro organization on Monday, a year almost to the day since the company received its first substantial defence contract, one calling for 124 aircraft for the RCAF. Since then not one has been delivered."[4]

The appointment might have come as a surprise to some, but not to the man who made it happen — C.D. Howe. "It was quite obvious that the management of the day was not likely to produce what we wanted," he would say years later. "The top management of A.V. Roe was a resident in England. The men on the job just did not have the experience necessary to carry out all the work."[5] It wouldn't be the first time C.D. Howe would display negative feelings towards A.V. Roe, one of his boys in charge or not.

Crawford Gordon had made a point of avoiding the ceremonial handing over and the subsequent return of the ill-fated CF-100 a couple of weeks before. Did he really know how bad things were? Probably. Any production man knows that taking an aircraft like the CF-100 from paper to production should have been done in half the time it had taken A.V. Roe. Showing up as company president *after* the deed had been done would convey a more positive message to the air force. Gordon arrived for his first day of work at A.V. Roe on November 1, 1951, but he didn't show up alone; with him came his secretary and confidant, Audrey Underwood.

His first act in his new job was to call Fred Smye into his office and ask him to assign someone to act as his temporary executive assistant, someone who had a good picture of the entire Malton organization, someone with a no-nonsense attitude. That person was Ron Adey.

"I probably knew more about the company, the people and the organization than anyone else," Adey would say years later. "There were probably other people who could have contributed a great deal more to him, but it would have disrupted the organization at a time when we were already being disrupted. He seemed to be most interested in the company's overall planning and scheduling activities and he appeared grossly involved in some 'external activities' before he got around to being involved in 'internal activities.'"[6]

Adey would stay with Gordon for about four months.

> *My job at A.V. Roe, said Gordon on his appointment, in a typical C.D. Howe manner, will be to organize, deputize and supervise. For nearly six years we've been designing, planning, testing and carrying on intricate research. We've achieved very ambitious objectives: two Canadian jet engines, a Jetliner, a Canadian jet fighter. The next step will be to produce them in quantity.[7]*

To a *Time* magazine reporter he was more to the point. "My primary job will be to get PRODUCTION, PRODUCTION, PRODUCTION!"[8] The bull had arrived in his china shop.

Within days, Gordon could see that the company Howe had given him to turn around was in bad shape; production lines had stopped and the returned CF-100s still sat on the tarmac, a visible slap in the face to the company that had made them. On November 2, he called Fred Smye and Paul Dilworth, the head of the Gas Turbine Division, into his office to discuss reorganizing the company. On November 8 he ordered the production of the Avro Jetliner prototype number two stopped, and closed a sales office the company had opened in New York in the hope of selling the plane to the Americans. The company, said Gordon, would concentrate on getting the CF-100 fixed and into production. After all, the company had been founded on the faith of its wartime activity and that's where the future would lie — in the production of military aircraft.

But first, how to fix the CF-100? Knowing he couldn't keep his old boss Howe at bay forever, he ordered Fred Smye to take the company's chief engineer, Edgar Atkin, to England to meet with the people at Hawker-Siddeley and find out a way to fix the plane. When Smye got to see Sir Roy Dobson, the welcome was less than lukewarm. He still wasn't sold on the idea of Crawford Gordon running his operation in Canada and, recalls Smye:

> commenced to giving me a going-over like I've never had either before or since. He couldn't understand why we were over here and thought it ridiculous we couldn't solve our own technical problems by ourselves. He then went on to say that the real problem with the CF-100 was myself and my Canadian friends in the RCAF. I also found out later he had told Walter Deischer that I was disloyal and had undermined his leadership.
>
> I was shocked. I kept telling Dobson that I couldn't handle the situation at Malton any longer and that I was going to resign. 'And I'm not going to resign to you because I don't work for you any more. I'm going to resign to Gordon.
>
> When I returned to Canada, I walked into Crawford's office and said, 'It's all yours boy, I'm through!' And I told him that Dobson blamed me for the CF-100 problems and said that

I had engineered them with the air force ... and that I was fed up.

After Crawford calmed me down, I told him I would stay with the aircraft side of the company, if neither he nor Dobson would stick their nose in it, that it's all mine, no interference whatsoever.

OK, Freddie, here's the deal, responded Gordon. I'll fix the company. You fix the plane![9]

* * * *

Mary Gordon was happy to have her husband home again and the family back together after eight long months in Ottawa. The Gordons moved to 159 Forest Hill Road in mid-Toronto and Gordon immediately enrolled Cynthia and Diana at Bishop Strachan, a private school for girls. Gordon never really believed in university education and thought the best education was reading, travelling and getting a job. Gordon's children were probably away from home more than their famous father during the 1950s. During the school months they were boarded out at schools including Ridley College for Crawford or Compton for Diana and Cynthia. Diana recalls being sent to five different schools: Branksome Hall, Compton (in Quebec), Bishop Strachan, Havergal and a single year of public education at Jarvis Collegiate in Toronto. Summers were no different. The kids were sent away to camp, usually Wapomeo or Ahmek in Algonquin Park.

But for Mary, at least, the family would be together for weekends and despite the long hours, she could finally count on her husband coming home almost every night. Or could she?

* * * *

Fred Smye began his job of fixing the aircraft by firing the company's chief engineer, Edgar Atkin, and promoting a close friend of his, James Charles Floyd, the father of the Avro Jetliner. Floyd had been with the company since March 1946 and had endeared himself to most everyone, was well liked and well respected. Born in Manchester, England in 1914, Floyd was in high school when the A.V. Roe company in that city started a program to train bright youngsters as company apprentices. It was a much coveted position and the competition for a place was intense. But Floyd had an uncle who was a friend of Roy Dobson's; he appealed to him to let Floyd into the program. "All right," barked Dobson to the 15-year-old, "but I don't know you from here on. You join the scheme, you're on your own entirely." It was January 1930.[10]

In the next four or five years, Floyd tried his hand at all sorts of jobs throughout the plant. When the company held a competition to allow successful apprentices to study engineering at university, Floyd won and entered the Manchester College of Technology, working nearly full-time at the plant while attending school. After graduating he joined Hawker Aircraft in its design office and worked on the Hawker Hotspur, an aircraft based on the famous Hurricane. By 1937 he was back at A.V. Roe in Manchester working on the Anson, the Manchester, the famous Lancaster and the York bomber. In 1945 Stuart Davies found Floyd and persuaded him to go to Canada to work at newly formed A.V. Roe Canada in Malton on the aircraft that would eventually become the Avro C-102 Jetliner. He arrived in Malton in January 1946.

Fred Smye promoted Jim Floyd from works manager to chief engineer in January 1952 and the very first thing Floyd did in his new job was to start up what informally became known as the "blitz group." It had one job: fix the CF-100, and fix it quickly.

"If there is no satisfactory solution of the present difficulties within the next two or three weeks," Howe would write to Gordon in December 1951, "we will have to consider abandoning the project. I am determined that if we can't get production as planned, we will get some other producer."[11]

The half dozen members of the blitz group immediately did a thorough investigation on one of the CF-100s returned by the RCAF. The investigation zeroed in on the plane's centre spar. A centre spar, critical to every aircraft, runs right through the width of the plane, supporting the wings and, in the case of the CF-100, its engines as well.

It appeared that it was flexing too much. It took six weeks for the blitz group to come up with a solution: a pin-joint concept with rein-forcement plates that would now allow the wing to flex, but would permit the engine cowling to flex along with it. The group also found other problems including some centre-section rib weaknesses and deficiencies in some of the structural components. It took the blitz group eight weeks to complete the work, and although the plane was now fixed, the CF-100 was also 400 lbs heavier. A cardinal rule had been breached; you never make an aircraft heavier.

Years later, Fred Smye claimed that about 4,300 different changes had been made to the plane, but Jim Floyd claims the figure was closer to 34,000. As one engineer would observe later, "It was like taking all the bones out of a chicken, fixing them, then putting them all back in."[12] On July 22, 1952, the CF-100 was redelivered to the air force, this time without ceremony, some eight months after being returned. In all, A.V. Roe would produce 692 of the aircraft.

Fred Smye had "fixed" the plane.

FIXING A.V. ROE

With the blitz group solving their problem, Crawford Gordon set out to solve his. By the end of January, he had written down a list of his essentials and priorities, not just for getting the CF-100 into produc-tion, but for the future of A.V. Roe. They turned out to be a remark-able combination of theories, beliefs and principles largely learned through his years in Ottawa with C.D. Howe. They touched on both industrial techniques and human relations.

He then hired the management-consulting firm of Price Waterhouse to test his beliefs, research the company and come up with a basic structure that would carry A.V. Roe to the end of the decade. Realiz-ing that aircraft and engines were separate products with potentially separate markets, his only stipulation was they remain separate divi-sions. The aircraft division would now be known as Avro Aircraft Ltd., and the engine division would take the name Orenda Engines

Ltd. after their famous engine. A.V. Roe Ltd. would now be known as A.V. Roe Canada Ltd. and function as a holding company.

Price Waterhouse completed their evaluation of the company and soon after, Gordon outlined in a speech to the Canadian Club in Toronto how it would look. No clearer example exists of Gordon's business philosophy and how A.V. Roe Canada would function as a corporation. It could just as easily have been written by C.D. Howe:

> *In this war we are now waging (and I use the word 'war' advisedly), the ideas, enthusiasm and drive produced by an enlightened management are weapons almost as effective as guns. The fact that I can talk to you tonight about 'management teamwork' in a defence plant is good proof to me of our eventual victory. I'll wager my life there is no similar meeting tonight in Soviet Russia.*
>
> *In the past 25 years the world has been in a constant state of turmoil. Commencing with the Depression in the early thirties which led up to the Second World War — the reconversion to peace and the advent of the Cold War — all these worldwide events have brought about social unrest and great changes. Economic shifts, the changes in standards of living, the uprooting of masses of people seem to have caused a general sense of dissatisfaction among people. This feeling seems to be prevalent in business today and highlights a very acute problem we all face — job dissatisfaction.*
>
> *I cannot stress too strongly the necessity for understanding — that the internal friction which is apparent in any large organization of capable executives can only be kept at a minimum if there is complete understanding and application of the organizational structure and authority. And it is on this subject I wish to speak to you tonight.*[13]

Sounding very much like he was talking about Munitions and Supply and the war years, Gordon continued:

What is meant by 'management teamwork' and how is it achieved? My definition is taken from the Three Musketeers — 'One for all and all for one.' You may ask how is this happy state of affairs brought about? I believe by attention and action to ensure:

1. *proper organization;*

2. *appointment of well-qualified personnel to key positions;*

3. *clear-cut definition of duties and responsibilities;*

4. *proper delegation of authority; and*

5. *aggressive internal communication programs to ensure that all employee are aware of policies and plans of the company.*

By proper organization I mean a plan of administration geared to the problem of a particular business or operation, a plan which clearly defines the objectives of the business.

The three common types of organization used today are functional, line and staff, but it is becoming increasingly apparent that in most large businesses, it is impossible to practice a single type of organization, and in many instances, it is necessary to combine these basic types.

We are all used to commenting on successful companies, but how many of us analyse the reason for this success. Successful organizations do not come about by chance, but are carefully planned. Some people believe that companies are usually built around one or two strong characters who dominate the organization. This may be true in a few small businesses, but in more complex companies, it is the responsibility of management to have a plan of organization and then fit the employees with the proper ability into the various jobs so that the entire structure is strong and lasting.

In many companies, policy dictates that money be spent in developing new facilities, new products or new businesses, and yet little is done to gear the old organization to the new concepts with a resultant loss of business and shrinkage of profit. This lack of foresight or initiative can be illustrated by the story of a traveller who while going through the backwoods, came across a squatter sitting in front of his cabin. He said: 'How's things?' The squatter replied, 'Everything's OK except my roof leaks.' 'Why don't you fix it?' 'Well, I can't when it's raining.' 'Why not fix it when it ain't raining?' 'It don't leak when it don't rain.'

The growth of a business venture is an evolution of methods and men. The process is accelerated in periods of extreme economic change, such as we are now going through, and management must be enlightened enough to continually review its objectives and bring about the necessary changes in order to meet these objectives.

The most important aspect of a successful organization is the flow of authority from level to level, commencing with the board of directors through the president and officers down to the operating levels.

Please pardon me if I illustrate by referring to my own company and how we have recently organized so that we may finally achieve maximum teamwork. Inasmuch as our activities embrace research, design and development, as well as production in two complex and rapidly changing fields — aircraft and turbo engines — I feel that our organization must be geared to the general principle just outlined and might serve as an example.

A new airplane does not just happen — it is the result of hundreds of thousands of hours of hard work by many types of skills. In the aircraft industry, engineering alone occupies an unique position in that all aspects of engineering knowledge are combined before a prototype can be built and take the air. The finished product is the result of the direction of a high degree of technical knowledge and superb craftsmanship. The technical staff besides the chief designer includes the aerodynamic expert, the stressman, the research worker, the armament expert, the technical engineer, the radar expert, the experimental test section including wind-tunnel analysis and finally, the test pilot. At Avro we have this task and in addi-

tion, the task of performing design, development research and production functions on jet engines with as many varied technical operations.

To weld these many varied technical occupations into a team is a task by itself, but the combination of such a group with an organization necessary to produce as well as develop, called for a particular type of organization to meet the problem. It also, by the nature of the very ramifications of the business, called for clean-cut authority and defined functional responsibility.

Our company has been using the functional-type organization which, while appropriate when we were wholly occupied in development work, was completely inadequate as soon as the government inaugurated a defence program and ordered production.

We therefore decided on a combination of the line- and staff-type of organization, feeling that properly balanced, one with the other, and completely understood by all, this organization was most suitable to the problem created by changing conditions. Two self-contained operating divisions were formed — an aircraft division and a gas turbine division, each under a general manager who is solely responsible to myself. It is made clear to these general managers that under the general policies of the company, they are charged with the responsibility of attaining the objectives specified in their approved budgets with regard to manufacturing schedules, engineering performance (both design and production) cost and profits. Each general manager has his own works manager, chief engineer, purchasing director, comptroller, quality control director, personnel manager, so that he is given control over the necessary working functions in order to achieve the objectives of the operation.

Under the by-laws of most companies, all duties are assigned to the president as the executive officer of the company. An organization cannot be a one-man operation and succeed. Accordingly, it is necessary for me to segregate my authority and pass it on to members of the organization by way of spe-

cific assignments, with titles indicating responsibility, the authority delegated to the position and the responsibility which must go with the authority.

In determining the policies of the company, in various fields, the president must have certain staff officers associated with him to whom he delegates a segment of his authority. In these fields I am talking of finance, industrial relations, public relations, sales and advertising and research and engineering.

These staff officers must of necessity be the best trained and most skilled in their particular fields. They must have a complete understanding of the difference between line and staff duties. The staff plans and teaches while the line executes. We therefore decided to organize with staff functions in the fields of sales and service, finance, industrial relations, public relations, research and engineering and facilities — and line functions in the two operating divisions (aircraft and gas turbine) feeling this type of organization was best suited to our problem of successful operation.

The general managers and the directors of the staff functions are members of a management committee which meets weekly to discuss various problems and decide on basic company policy. Each director is given a clear-cut definition of his responsibility and the scope of his authority. This responsibility and authority is agreed in committee with the general managers, whose operating role has already been outlined and is understood by the directors.

This discussion and development of ideas in this democratic fashion assures that the management is agreed on a basis of operation. It is extremely important that management then inform their staff of company policy and lead them to the same goal set for all division and department heads.

In order to achieve this, a communications program is necessary which can be best launched with a company paper, a proper industrial-relations program, frequent staff meetings at which supervisors take their employees into their confidence, company balance sheets being explained to all personnel, labour management committees and many other devices.

Management teamwork can be achieved and its effect on morale and operating efficiency can be great. An example of this application can be told in connection with the second flight of our Jetliner. The plane had to crash-land because of a failure of its hydraulics system, which of course has since been corrected. Most aircraft would be written off after such a crash landing, but the Jetliner, because of its sturdy construction, was flying again in a couple of weeks. That it flew so soon was largely due to the voluntary action of hundreds of employees who returned from their summer holidays without being told, ready to work and to repair the damage.

We are a young organization, organized only some six years ago, but we have grown quickly. We started with a bare floor, a handful of employees and a few ideas. Today there are some 9,000 of us and when we get into full production soon, there will probably be 15,000 of us, one of the largest working forces in Canada. Since Korea, we have had to expand our facilities considerably so that now we have more than a million and a half square feet of floor space on some 350 acres of property. Among the new buildings is a self-contained jet manufacturing plant, which should be a great help to the present worldwide shortage of vitally needed engines. Because of the seriousness of the international situation, these production facilities were rushed to completion within a year. Although every effort was made to save money and obtain the maximum facilities with minimum of expense, this plant is comparable to anything in the world.

The switch from a development to a production organization has involved tremendous problems for us, which have only been solved by teamwork from the top down, or in certain areas, from the bottom up. Work procedures had to be organized while designs were made and jigs and tools set up. The search for required engineering and technical personnel has been a problem in itself. There has been a constant switching of departments and locations, imposing poor working conditions for everyone concerned. Morale, however, has remained high.

Avro Canada is an independent member of the Hawker-Sid-deley Group, the largest aircraft and engine manufacturer in the world, and because of this, can offer another illustration of teamwork. We pride ourselves that we are an independent Canadian company, but like Canada itself, we also pride ourselves in our British connection. The Group is a marvellous organization, a sort of General Motors in aviation. Member companies pool their knowledge but at the same time, often compete with each other in friendly rivalry.

At Avro Canada we believe that a company functions best when every employee, from chairman of the board to sweeper, understands his part in the mission of the company; and further understands fully how and when his part is to be played and what he is to accomplish. No person or organization can amount to much unless he or it sets an ultimate goal. And the best way to achieve this goal in a big organization, we think, is to make it clear and obvious to all just what the goal is and keep everyone up to date on the tactics employed from time to time to achieve that goal.

We believe this policy will pay off and if it does, management teamwork, with the high morale brought about by achievement, will do a lot to preserve our way of life.[14]

* * * *

To many at A.V. Roe, Crawford Gordon's arrival was the breath of fresh air everyone had been waiting for. "Gordon was so different in character from Deischer that the change in management was almost startling," writes Jim Floyd.

On the day after he arrived, he got all of the executives together and demanded a detailed rundown on the status of all activities in the company. Within weeks he had reviewed and revised the management structure and we were all quite clear on what we were expected to do. Much has been written about Crawford Gordon's character and aggressive approach, some of it derogatory and critical of his methods in dealing with people and the government. It is quite true that Gordon would not 'suffer fools' easily or accept a weak approach to anything, and if one made a serious mistake, he could be ruthless and unbending. But he was also quick to praise and help those whom he felt were genuinely doing their best and working for the good of the company. I wish to go on record in saying that I personally found it exciting and rewarding to work for and with Crawford Gordon. He was a man who knew what he wanted and would not hesitate to move the earth to get it, but I believe that it was all in the interest of A.V. Roe and Canada in general.[15]

Some people saw another side of the new president. "Crawford appeared cold and distant only because he was shy," recalls one of Avro's former executive secretaries.

People didn't think he was friendly, but he was basically quite warm and it showed through his friendships; the few close friends he had were long-time friendships. And he always talked about making things happen, about bringing about a success. He had little patience with people who talked all the time. Even the way he walked, he stood straight; he chaired management meetings straight but he was always impatient. He would always cut people off.[16]

He was so dynamic, recalls another. He could look at an annual report and read it in a flash. He intimidated people and I remember he got really fed up whenever he was cornered by people, in a hallway, at a social, anywhere.

But he was cute. He had that little-boy quality about him that is so attractive in men.[17]

But to many of the thousands of employees in the assembly bays and offices, he would remain a tall, balding, distant figure with little to say. He very rarely appeared in the assembly bays. For him to go out there and say "Hi guys!" was not, in his opinion, going to do much for his day. And to those who questioned his understanding of the aircraft industry, he would say:

> *I don't need to know the aircraft industry — one industry is the same as another — it takes the same things to make a successful corporation, to make it profitable or unprofitable. I don't need to know how the wings go on the fuselage.*[18]

In the beginning, running Avro didn't worry Gordon a lot, recalls his first assistant Ron Adey, because he basically delegated everything.[19]

When Gordon arrived at A.V. Roe he wasn't alone. Soon after joining the company he asked two of his former colleagues from the John Inglis days to join him. Bill Dickie came in as head of the company's Industrial Relations in November and later, in October 1953, Walter McLachlan became the general manager of Orenda Engines. And, of course, there was Audrey. The company newsletter once featured an article on her:

> *In reply to the question of what it's like working for the boss, Audrey pointed out that it was mostly a case of being prepared for any eventuality and trying to establish answers before the questions are asked! That doesn't exactly sound easy. Mr. Gordon, as we are coming to realize, is dynamic to say the least, and of course his tempo in no small way affects that of his secretary. Audrey does not appear to be lacking in this respect as she vigorously pursues the variety of duties that befall one of such a position. She says Mr. Gordon has a wonderful sense of humour and makes great decisions quickly and wisely.*
>
> *In the hobby department, Audrey specializes in tennis, swimming, golf, badminton, skiing and sewing.*[20]

Audrey had quite a sense of humour herself. Her friend Jean Taylor recalls the time she and Audrey attended a performance of the National Ballet Company at the O'Keefe Centre in Toronto. Because the two ladies both loved the ballet, they had good seats close to the orchestra and stage. During a particularly serious scene, a number of male dancers pranced out on the stage to perform a routine. Their arrival startled Audrey and she began to giggle and couldn't stop, much to Jean's embarrassment. Her laughter was so infectuous that, before long, she had the entire audience laughing so uncontrollably that the performance had to be stopped.[21]

Today the Canadian aviation industry, like the airplane itself, is here to stay, Gordon would say in his first pronouncement to the company's employees in early 1952. In the coming years it will have a most beneficial effect on Canadian economy, on Canadian life and on Canada's small population. Canada is now the third democratic air power and the airplane is playing a leading role in opening up the underdeveloped regions of our country. Our aviation industry, which has just come of age, has a very real future, not only in supplying our own-designed aircraft and engines for the RCAF and our own airlines, but because of their proven quality for export use as well.

… Every aircraft flying great circle routes between Europe or Asia and the United States must fly over Canada and the Arctic. Obviously Canada will benefit enormously from this strategic geographic location, provided the world remains at peace.

Aircraft now being made to train Canadian aircrew, as well as the aircrew of NATO countries, will, to a certain extent, allow Canada to take over its last war role as the 'airdrome of democracy.'

Avro Canada today, like other Canadian aviation firms, is much more than an arms factory, but a veritable arsenal for peace. The company is most anxious to play a leading part in the larger more constructive task of improving Canada's economic, peacetime potential.

Avro Canada is the heart and brains for the whole country's new jet aircraft and engine industry.[22]

HOWARD HUGHES AND THE AVRO JETLINER

C.D. Howe wasted little time in seeing how his Boy Wonder was doing at Malton, and despite the company's efforts in "fixing" the CF-100 and getting it into production, the minister wouldn't let up on his feelings about the company's "other" project: Jim Floyd's C-102 Jetliner.

> *One of the events which I remember during that period was the visit of C.D. Howe to Malton, recalls Jim Floyd, apparently for the purpose of convincing himself that Avro was doing everything possible to get the CF-100 delivered to the RCAF. I was introduced to him as the new works manager, and during the introduction, Fred Smye mentioned that I was the chief designer on the Jetliner. Howe turned to me and said, 'I suggest that you forget that airplane and put your energy into getting the CF-100s out!' I said nothing, but my thoughts would have turned the room blue! This was the only time that I had ever met Howe, despite his tremendous influence throughout the course of the Jetliner project, and as I drove home that night I couldn't help thinking how ironic it was that after a dedicated team had worked their hearts out on the project for over five years and produced that world-beating aircraft, all he could say was 'forget it.' But then I never did understand politicians.*[23]

On trips to the plant, Howe always seemed to have something negative to say about the Jetliner, but the strangest of his remarks would come years later when asked to comment on the plane by a *Globe and Mail* reporter. "We brought it to the prototype stage," said Howe. "And while it is true it flew, there was everything wrong with it. It had to carry sand in the tail to fly."[24] Even Gordon felt he had to respond to this one. "I don't understand his remark," he said. "He knows full well the Jetliner met the Department of Transport specifications in every detail. It was shelved at the outbreak of the Korean War only because Avro was asked to concentrate on defence work [the CF-100]. It's still in service as a flying laboratory. It is a good plane."[25]

But was the minister merely using the Jetliner to hide deeper concerns?

"Have you ever heard of a company that's got too much on its plate?" Howe once asked a company official. "Well that's Avro!"[26]

But if Canada didn't want the Jetliner, maybe the Americans did. In late spring of 1952, Gordon was having a few drinks with Bob Rummell of Trans World Airlines (TWA) whose owner was the infamous Howard Hughes. The Hughes Aircraft Company of Culver City, California had the contract to supply the MG-2 fire-control system for the CF-100. Despite grumbling that the plane was the most expensive flying laboratory in existence, Gordon raved about the Jetliner to Rummell and eventually Hughes himself wanted to have a look at it. Knowing Howe's sensitivity about the Jetliner, Gordon suggested sending the plane to California under the guise of using it as a camera platform to film the testing of Hughes's MG-2. After all, the aircraft could easily take off and fly to 35,000 ft in relative comfort and could fly fast enough to keep up with the CF-100.

The Jetliner and crew arrived in Culver City on April 7 for what would become the strangest period in the life of the aircraft controlled, in large part, by Howard Hughes himself. "The day after we got there," recalls Jetliner pilot Don Rogers, "Hughes came around and looked at the airplane with interest and wanted to have a flight in it and have me check him out on it. We changed seats and he did about nine take-offs and landings. But when he landed for the last time, instead of taxing back to the Hughes factory side of the landing strip, he taxied over to the other side of the airstrip. He put cars and guards around the plane and that was the last Hughes Aircraft ever got to see of the plane. They never did use it or even look at it as a flying test bed."[27] Howard Hughes, it seemed, had found himself a new toy.

Crawford Gordon and Fred Smye had gone ahead and had taken over an entire floor of the Beverly Hills Hotel in Los Angeles, thinking negotiations with Hughes over the aircraft might take a few days. The hotel would end up being Fred Smye's home for the next six months.

I remember my first meeting with Hughes, recalls Fred Smye. I was told to go out of the back door of the hotel, cross the lawn to the side street, where I would find the green Chevy and Hughes. I drove with him to the Hughes plant, where an old Convair aircraft with a rusty undercart was parked. There was a mechanic standing by the plane with a fire extinguisher. We got in, although you could hear my knees shaking a mile away. Howard got the engines started but not the pressurization system and, fortunately, because of that, we could not fly. That was when he gave me a conducted tour of his properties and borrowed a dollar from me to buy some gas, as the tank of the Chevy was almost dry.[28]

In the back of their minds, however, Gordon and Smye looked forward to dealing with Howard Hughes as he owned TWA and might purchase some aircraft which, in turn, might resurrect the Jetliner program at Malton. And get C.D. Howe off their backs.

Despite considerable wining and dining over the next few weeks during which Gordon would claim years later that he had actually seen movie star Rita Hayworth naked, Gordon's patience with Hughes was quickly wearing thin. "The cloak-and-dagger atmosphere surrounding Hughes, and his elusiveness," recalls Jim Floyd, "... were completely alien to Gordon's own direct and positive approach to anything in which he was involved. It was well known that his patience with any other approach was not inexhaustible."[29]

During one set of discussions Hughes excused himself to go to the bathroom. When 90 minutes went by, Gordon became quite agitated and demanded to know what was going on. When he was told that Hughes was on the telephone in the bathroom, Gordon went ballistic.

"I will not repeat the exact comment that this revelation brought from Crawford," writes Jim Floyd, "but he left the penthouse almost immediately, muttering about a 'bloody madhouse'."[30]

The next night Gordon got a chance to pay back the discourtesy. "Gordon usually smoked and drank his way through these evening meetings — to the endless irritation of Hughes — and was presently in need of a washroom himself.

'Howard,' he demanded, 'Where's the can?'
'The washroom is down the hall,' said Hughes.
'What's the matter with the can right here?' Gordon pointed to Hughes's private washroom adjacent to the suite.
'That's my special washroom to be used only by myself; you can use the one down the hall.'

But before Hughes could stop him, Gordon was in Hughes's bathroom with the door locked. The next day Hughes discovered that, out of spite, Gordon had purposely urinated everywhere but the toilet."[31]

Soon after that incident Gordon flew home, leaving the negotiating to his calmer lieutenant, Fred Smye. But despite the six-month sojourn in California, Howard Hughes never did buy the Jetliner. For years Hughes would call Gordon at all hours of the day and night and ramble on about the Jetliner and how much he loved it. More often than not, Gordon would refuse to talk to Hughes, leaving Mary or one of the children to field the calls.

Howe continued to remain under fire in the House of Commons over A.V. Roe. With the CF-100 production line restarted, the criticisms centred mostly around the heavy government investments in the young company. To date over $120 million had been spent and not one CF-100 was in the air over Canadian skies. But knowing Crawford Gordon was now in charge seemed to appease Howe somehow. "It is a relief to have management in charge which appreciates that a problem exists and is prepared to tackle it with energy and dispatch," he would write to Gordon in March 1952.[32] And again in July, "I congratulate you on having placed your company in a sound financial position. I see no reason why Avro cannot be established as an independent company and become a real competitor of Canadair."[33]

Media interest in the young company and its president was forcing Gordon into the spotlight more and more, a position with which he was not entirely comfortable. It was one thing making speeches in C.D. Howe's place, but now Gordon was on the defensive, having to explain Avro's problems to the demanding media. He hated that. In a few short months, the company had become one of the country's largest employers with 12,000 people on the payroll and hiring at the rate of 30 per day. The media scrutiny could only intensify as more and more attention was given to the company that was quickly changing the face of Canadian aviation.

During one particular interview, Gordon openly criticized *The Globe and Mail*'s aviation writer Jim Hornick over a story he had written about a new aircraft the company was working on. This aircraft was state of the art, was supposed to fly supersonically and had a radical new delta shape.

"It so happens," denied Gordon to the press, "that we are not working on such a project...."[34]

But, it so happened, they were.

THE GENESIS OF THE CF-105 AVRO ARROW

Canada has never had a very orderly process for the procurement or replacement of its military hardware due in part to financing issues, the military itself and the fact that we are basically an unmilitary country. On one side of the fence is the military, the chiefs of staff, who had been accustomed in the past to simply submitting their equipment shopping lists to Cabinet for consideration with absolutely no thought of the political implications of their request. "We don't attempt to please the politicians," said former Air Vice Marshall John Easton, "only to satisfy the defence requirement at the time."[35]

On the other side of the procurement fence are the elected officials, the politicians, usually men and women with very little understanding of military affairs. They know equipment is important for the defence of Canada, but what kind of equipment, and will the purchase of that equipment determine defence policy for years to come?

Between the politician and the military lie the defence contractors who, when a particular type of military equipment is not available could find themselves in the position of both designing and manufacturing that piece of equipment. Should problems arise in the design stage — which are inevitable when dealing with something as complex as state-of-the-art aircraft — those problems quickly translate into delays. Delays mean that costs escalate; escalating costs mean political problems; and political problems mean pressure on the defence contractor to get the equipment into production and into the hands of the military as soon as possible — sometimes sooner than they should. This was what happened with the CF-100.

Even before the CF-100 had been finally delivered to the RCAF in 1952, air force defence planners were already looking ahead to the next generation of aircraft to meet any threat to the defence of Canada and North America. In the late 1940s and well into the 1950s, the immediate threat was an aerial attack by Soviet bombers flying over the polar ice cap. The idea for the aircraft that would eventually be known as the CF-105 Avro Arrow began as a result of this Soviet threat.

The decision for a specific type of air defence or aircraft came about through a series of steps, or procurement procedures, which the RCAF in those days liked to call "Plan H." The first step involved collecting as much information as possible from our allies on the immediate and long-range threat to the defence of continental North America. This information was then passed on to the military planners in both the RCAF and the Defence Research Board (DRB). Collectively they determined how Canada's armed forces could jointly plan a course of action and identify the necessary military hardware to meet the threat. If the required equipment was not available, the RCAF Operational Requirements staff (OR) would draw up a set of preliminary specifications for the necessary aircraft, which would include general aircraft capabilities and performance. The RCAF OR staff in those days consisted of two or three eager young guys with engineering degrees and some knowledge of aerodynamics and thrust to weight ratios, elements necessary in understanding modern aircraft.

A typical Operational Requirement would consist of two or three pages on an aircraft's expected performance; although the OR staff would "ask for the stars," they usually also based their request on something within the current state of the art and not entirely in "never-never land."[36] They would ask for the fastest, highest and deadliest but tried to make certain it was doable. The OR then went to the Air Council for approval, then to the Chiefs of Staff and then to the Department of Defence for money for development costs if an "off-the-shelf" aircraft could not meet the requirements. Then the Department of Supply and Services tendered the OR to foreign and domestic aircraft companies. Those interested consulted their own engineers as to whether they could produce what was requested. If they felt confident, the company submitted a design proposal to Supply and Services and if the bid was accepted, a development contract was awarded, usually for the production of one or two prototype aircraft. A company/RCAF liaison team was set up and if the air force was happy with the results, a production contract was awarded to produce a certain number of aircraft over a certain period of time at a unit cost per plane. The company then proceeded to:

- hire personnel;
- order jigs, tools and fixtures;
- build wooden mock-ups;
- manufacture the necessary parts;
- sub-assemble the plane;
- assemble the prototypes;
- establish flight trials;
- establish proving runs;
- roll-out the aircraft;
- conduct the first flight;
- award the production contract; and
- deliver to RCAF for squadron use.

Even before the CF-100 was delivered to the RCAF, the air force was already considering the type of aircraft that would replace it. The company had looked into a swept-wing version of the CF-100, but had abandoned the attempt when air-tunnel tests proved it to be barely supersonic. Former Air Vice Marshall (AVM) John Easton was instrumental in creating a program after the Second World War that encouraged young air force officers with university degrees to take upgrading in state-of-the-art aviation technology. A number of these young officers served on OR staff and one of them, Deac Bray, was given the job of studying advanced aerodynamics, and to look at the most likely configuration of what the aircraft that would follow the CF-100 would look like.

"Bray went to the States, Britain and France," reveals Easton, "and all through the industry and put down his report. In it he outlined an airplane that had the configuration of a tailless delta-winged aircraft. Now this was in 1948 and the general thinking of our boys in the back room. It was Bray's report that let us know what the future airplane should look like."[37] That report became the Operational Requirement Air-7-3 that resulted in the Avro Arrow.

"The Air staff," writes Jim Floyd, "had asked for the moon. They required a two-place (pilot and navigator) twin-engined aircraft with all-weather reliability, long range, short take-off and landing, an internal weapons compartment as large as the bomb bay of the B-29 and a supersonic manoeuvrability of 2 g at Mach 1.5 at 50,000 ft without any loss in speed or altitude — a requirement which has been met by few, if any, service aircraft even to this day. In addition, it was to be guided by the most sophisticated automatic flight and fire control system ever envisaged. It was small wonder [that the RCAF] team had failed to find any such aircraft on the drawing boards anywhere in the world."[38]

In July 1953 the Department of Defence Production authorized Avro Aircraft to carry out a design study for an aircraft to meet the requirement. Following a comprehensive evaluation of Avro's proposal, the RCAF then issued a design and development contract to the company in the spring of 1954.

Originally, the CF-105 was designed around a Rolls Royce engine known as the RB-106, but that engine program was cancelled, forcing Avro to switch to an American engine — the Curtiss-Wright J-67 — only to have the US government pull out its support for it. The company then decided to use the Pratt and Whitney J-75 in the early version and fit the later aircraft with an engine currently under development at the company's Orenda Engine plant. This new engine would later be known as the Iroquois. Within two years since Crawford Gordon took over A.V. Roe, the company was involved in two very risky projects: the design and development of a state-of-the-art airframe and a state-of-the-art engine.

And no one was more cognizant of this than C.D. Howe. Even though his Boy Wonder was now in charge, Howe never really trusted A. V. Roe's capabilities to deliver on expectation, at least on the aircraft side. The CF-100 had scared him; the Jetliner had soured him and the Arrow terrified him.

I understand that your department is planning a substantial development program for new supersonic jet engines and for a new fighter aircraft, he would write to his Cabinet colleague, Defence Minister Brooke Claxton. Before authorizing these items, I think you should appreciate what has already been spent on the Orenda Engine and the CF-100 to date. I must say I am frightened for the first time in my Defence Production experience. I would argue that at least a year be allowed to pass before any further development work at Avro is undertaken…

I must tell you that the design staff at Avro is far from competent to undertake work of this importance. Their designing record to date is very bad indeed, measured by any standard. If we must have further development work, let us contract it with a British firm which has the personnel, equipment and experience that qualifies them to do work of this kind. Someone so equipped can do the work for a fraction of the cost involved in making the attempt at A.V. Roe.

I hope you will give serious consideration to the dangers inherent in worsening our financial position at A.V. Roe.…[39]

PUBLIC RELATIONS

By early 1953 the company had orders on the books averaging $4 million per month, sometimes reaching as high as $9 million, largely to overhaul CF-100s, but was dependent on over 400 subcontractors and other companies for components and services. Not only was it continuing to produce CF-100s and Orenda engines, the company was involved in a number of aircraft overhaul projects for the RCAF. It was also the first year it turned a profit which Gordon used to purchase the Orenda Engine plant from the government for $17 million. The business of consolidation had begun.

"Acquisition of this plant," said Gordon on the purchase, "brings the whole Malton aircraft and engine operation under the private ownership of A. V. Roe Canada."[40] In his exuberance over the purchase, Gordon mentioned to his mentor that the company's engine, the Orenda, might find a market in the United States.

> *No, responded Howe, your full capacity is required for the Canadian aircraft program and therefore, you have nothing to sell. It would be a great comfort to me if you could give Parliament and the public the impression that all efforts of A.V. Roe are being devoted to carrying out the contracts you have in hand.*[41]

In other words, you've got enough on your plate Crawford. Concentrate on producing CF-100s and the Orenda to power it.

And when Gordon invited Howe to participate in the official reopening of the Orenda plant, now as A.V. Roe Canada's property, the minister would only agree to attend if none of the company's English partners were allowed to speak at the ceremony. As well, he would write Gordon, "I would hesitate to tell the world that we are making aircraft history with the opening of Canada's first engine plant, for any such representation might lead to unfortunate arguments with other manufacturers."[42] The minister, it seemed, was still smarting over the CF-100 delays. When Sir Roy Dobson heard of this, he directed his anger at Gordon, accusing him of being anti-British, anti-Group and other such things.

Despite almost alienating his mentor C.D. Howe and his immediate boss Sir Roy Dobson, the opening of the engine plant went well, but it also indicated that the company would have to spend a good deal more time on its public relations. Gordon himself did not like talking to the press; he mistrusted them and had no patience with their questioning. The two key aviation writers at the time, Bill Stephenson at *The Toronto Star* and Jim Hornick with *The Globe and Mail*, were seasoned journalists who knew how to get to the heart of a story. It had been the investigative work that Hornick had done, for instance, that had made the problems with the CF-100 aircraft public and had resulted in Crawford Gordon being hired in the first place.

With newspapers dedicating more and more of their time to covering what was going on at Malton — A.V. Roe Canada was *the* aviation news at the time in Canada — the company's management committee, on the urging of Avro Manager Fred Smye, decided to pay more attention to improving the company's public relations image. They approached a well-known Toronto advertising and public relations firm — Cockfield-Brown — to take on the project, and they specifically asked for one Brown employee. His name was J.N. "Pat" Kelly.

In earlier times power was measured by closeness to the prince and in any organization, there is always a shadow to the president. The function of such men goes back in history to the days when the title was chamberlain to the king. Some of these were simply valets who arranged the king's time as others would arrange his clothes or toiletries. But others were the traffic managers at the crossroads of decision making. Pat Kelly was the traffic manager — he decided what Gordon should pay attention to, who he should see and what would land on his desk. It was a function he would perform for the next seven years.

"Kelly had influence in Ottawa," recalls writer Jim Hornick. "But most of all, he had influence with Gordon."[43]

Pat Kelly had been a well-known journalist in the 1930s as the financial editor of the Vancouver *Sun* and in 1933, he founded the Vancouver *News-Herald*. He was the first Canadian newspaperman featured in a *Time* magazine story written by the famous American war correspondent Ernie Pyle.

In 1941 he joined Cockfield-Brown and was immediately seconded as national public relations director for the Canadian Red Cross for the duration of the war. After the war he was offered senior positions with Coca-Cola, Seagrams, the Brewers Association and his old company Cockfield-Brown. He agreed to join the firm but only if they let him set up his own public relations division, which they did.

In early 1952 over dinner, Gordon had complained to Kelly about the problems with the CF-100, his strained relationship with C.D. Howe, his dislike of the press and how his company was becoming more and more a target for the Conservative Opposition, which never seemed to stop trying to dig up dirt on Avro. Could Kelly help?

"Gordon wanted to borrow me for six months ... so I took the job half-time," recalls Kelly, "the idea being I would work at Malton mornings and back at my office in the afternoons. The day after I started, Gordon appointed me as a member of the management committee, which didn't sit too well with some, including Fred Smye. I very seldom spoke at these meetings, but I briefed Gordon before all of them. One of the very first suggestions I ever made to him was that it might be a good idea to start projecting the company as a Canadian company. I felt that since A. V. Roe's only customer was the Canadian government, we should forget about the English relationship and concentrate on the Canadian taxpayer. Gordon agreed to this immediately."[44]

As well as being responsible for writing all of Gordon's speeches, Kelly would also be free to advise the company's chairman of the board as well. "My whole approach was to function much like a lawyer does," recalls Kelly. "I would put before Gordon the possibilities he could do in a given situation but I made it clear to him that *he* makes the decision; his name goes on it and not mine."[45]

Because of this, very few people knew exactly what Kelly did. He was never quoted in the press, never gave interviews to the company's newsletters or spoke at board meetings or to any of the employees in general. But he always seemed to be close by, the chamberlain to Crawford Gordon, and he quickly earned the nickname "Grey Eminence" or "Gordon's Shadow." Before long Gordon wanted his "shadow" around on a full-time basis. "I was making $30,000 in those days," recalls Kelly, "and Gordon offered me a five-year contract at three times what I was making, plus a full pension. I refused. 'You stupid bastard,' he said, 'why won't you take it?' 'Loyalty,' I said, 'to Cockfield-Brown. They've been good to me.' 'Well you're still a stupid bastard.'"[46] But despite the occasional acrimonious comment, Gordon had full trust in Pat Kelly and would have for the next six years. "I had the full confidence of Crawford Gordon," Kelly would say years later. "Any decision I made had his approval."[47]

* * * *

By 1953, if Crawford Gordon wanted to talk business, he could do so in a number of locations. First was his office at Malton. On many occasions, the company's business was conducted over drinks at either the Toronto or York Clubs in Toronto. If the business was personal, however, it would be conducted at the company's private estate, Briarcrest, which was located on the south-west corner of Islington Avenue and Dixon Road in Toronto, a short six-mile drive from the Malton plant.

When Walter Deischer joined A.V. Roe in 1946 as its first president, he purchased the 11-acre parcel of land with its Tudor-style home as his residence. The house was beautiful and contained a huge living room with pegged oak-plank floors and a balcony above the front door. Beside the stone fireplace along one wall was a sliding panel door that led down into a recreation/pool room/bar area. The house had five bedrooms, two full bathrooms, two washrooms, a two-car garage and air conditioning. The wooded grounds contained a tennis court; it was an ideal location for company executive meetings and other corporate uses. When Deischer left the company on Gordon's arrival, it paid him $80,000 for the estate and Dobson brought two of his household employees from England to run the place.

At first only Sir Roy Dobson used the estate as his residence on his twice-yearly trips to Canada, but later the company billeted several potential customers there including, on many occasions, Prince Bernhard of the Netherlands and Viscount Montgomery from Great Britain. Even C.D. Howe stayed there from time to time, but more and more the company used the place for dinners and committee meetings. The food was excellent and the bar in the basement was always fully stocked. "When Crawford Gordon took over A.V. Roe," recalls Dorothy Smye, Fred Smye's former wife, "the company became much more social."[48] Briarcrest certainly played a part in this.

* * * *

1953 was not without personal challenges for Crawford Gordon. The first involved losing someone from his past; the second involved losing someone from his present. In April, Gordon's surrogate father and former headmaster at Appleby, John Guest died at his home in Nova Scotia. Although they had had little or no contact in the intervening years, Gordon never forgot the man. Without telling anyone, Gordon took a few days off and quietly went to the funeral. It was while staying in Halifax that Gordon heard of a corporation for sale that would become another member of the A.V. Roe family within five years. The company was the Dominion Steel and Coal Corporation, better known as Dosco.

While Gordon was in Halifax, someone close to him decided she no longer wanted to be close to him. Audrey Underwood figured it was time to leave the man she loved, more to save herself than for any other reason. Not being able to have Gordon on her terms had become unbearable. The relationship that had begun in Ottawa had carried over to Malton but not with the intensity of those first days at Defence Production in 1951. "You could watch the two of them in a room," recalled a friend years later, "and you could sense the electricity between them. Lots of electricity."[49] On at least two occasions company personnel had stumbled on them in Gordon's inner office in the most compromising of positions. Occasionally, they'd steal away for a weekend of skiing, but these times became rarer and rarer as Gordon's company grew around him at Malton and his family grew around him at home.

"Although Audrey liked a drink, she came to hate his drinking more and more," recalls the friend. "He had a sort of a drinking pattern. He wouldn't drink at all for quite a while and then something would

Karsh Portrait of Crawford Gordon II.

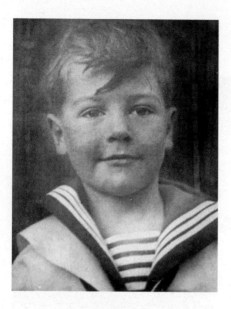

Crawford Gordon at 7: Crawford was a student in Miss Beckwith's private school in Kingston, Jamaica in 1921. He would live in Jamaica for 6 years.

Crawford Gordon at 11: The summer of his second year as an "Appleby Boy" in 1926.

Crawford Gordon at 21: June 1936, Crawford graduates with a Bachelor of Commerce degree from McGill University in Montreal. Below this photograph, in the yearbook, was his favourite saying, "Let's Go!"

Appleby College Football Team 1930: Crawford, 15, sits front row, second from the right. The school's yearbook praised him as a "first class half". Even then, Crawford appears as though he is sitting apart from everyone else.

20-Year-Old Mary Tierney: A Globe and Mail photographer caught Mary while relaxing at a debutante's ball in Toronto in November 1935.

Tierney Women 1920: Four-year-old Mary (middle) poses with her mother, Josephene, and older sister, Doris. Doris would tragically die at age 24 before Mary was out of her teens, leaving her an only child.

Tierney/Gordon Wedding, September 1936: Mary Tierney marries Crawford after a brief courtship. Crawford proposed to Mary after dating for only two weeks. "He wouldn't let up on me," she would say years later. "I liked his style!"

(Above) Four Key Players 1958: From the engineering side of the Arrow program are: (L to R) Bob Lindley, Jim Floyd, Guest Hake and Jim Chamberlin. When the program collapsed, Lindley went to McDonnell Douglas in California, Floyd returned to A.V. Roe in Manchester, Hake stayed on at Malton and Chamberlin headed up NASA's Gemini program.

(Left) Orenda Engines Plant Tour, September 1952: (L to R) Crawford Gordon, Sir Roy Dobson, Minister C.D. Howe observing assembly of the famous Orenda Engine.

CF-100 Enters Squadron Use — Late 1950s: Early production problems nearly spelled doom for A.V. Roe Canada. Gordon was appointed CEO by Howe in October 1951 to fix the company and get the CF-100 into production.

Avro C-102 Jetliner Flying Over New York City on April 18, 1950: The Jetliner was A.V. Roe Canada's other "tragedy". Only one copy of the Jetliner was made and it was cut up for scrap in 1956.

The Production Line: CF-100s on the production line at Avro Aircraft, a division of A.V. Roe Canada.

King Edward Hotel, 1957: Mary Gordon and Fred Smye chatting at company formal. Smye's wife at the time commented that A.V. Roe became more "social" after Crawford arrived.

12-Year-Old Cynthia Gordon Assists Her Father: Joan Gow, A.V. Roe employee, won a brand new automobile in a draw held at an Avro inter-squad game at Maple Leaf Gardens in February 1954.

Arrow Roll-Out, October 4, 1957: (L to R) Crawford Gordon III, Crawford Gordon, Mary Gordon, and friend.

Three Giants at the Arrow Roll-Out on October 4, 1957: (L to R) Sir Roy Dobson of Hawker-Siddeley Group, John A.D. McCurdy, and Crawford Gordon, with the Arrow as a back-drop. Dobson, at one time, had looked upon Crawford as a son.

Autumn 1958: A great shot of Arrow RL-204 landing at Malton with air brakes deployed. This aircraft only flew 8 times between October 1958 and February 1959, for a total flight time of 7 hours.

Crawford and Billie on Their Honeymoon, July 1959: A week before Crawford had been fired as CEO of A.V. Roe Canada.

19-Year-Old Billie Raphael (1941): Looking very Veronica Lake-like here, Billie gained membership into Hollywood's cafe society through her husband's close friend, actor Errol Flynn.

Billie Raphael, 1942 Hollywood: 20-year-old Billie poses for famous Hollywood star photographer, Hurriel. Eighteen years later she caught the eye of Crawford Gordon.

Summer 1960: Billie and Crawford on the lawn of their estate on Lexington Avenue in Montreal's Westmount. One of the last of the happier times in Montreal.

Westmount Estate, Summer 1960: Crawford relaxing playing table tennis in the games room of his estate. Although the owner of two businesses at this time, he spent much of his time at home.

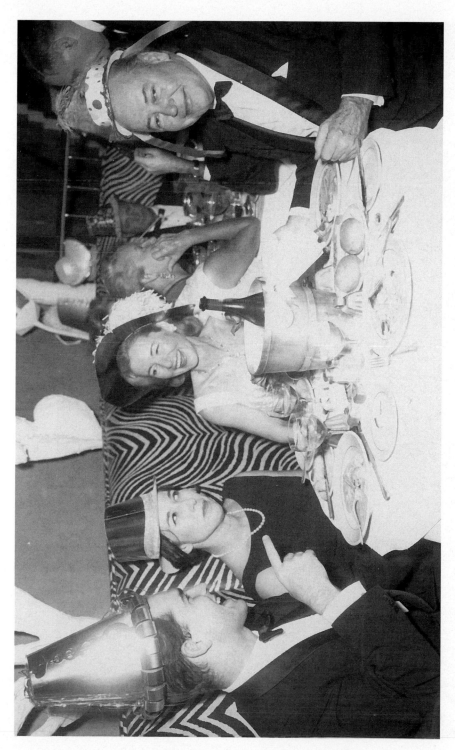

Partying at Maxim's in Paris, 1961: (L to R) Crawford's step-son, Stephen Raphael, friend of Stephen's, Billie Gordon, and Crawford Gordon celebrate New Year's Eve 1961.

March 25, 1958, First Flight of Arrow RL-201: In the background appears the massive Avro Aircraft Company in Malton. Less than a year later the Arrow program was cancelled, throwing over 14,500 men and women out of work. This first flight lasted about 20 minutes.

happen and he'd drink far too much. A personal thing at home; a crisis at work, and then he'd go to Briarcrest and he wouldn't go home for two or three days and he'd just drink all the time."[50]

"You know he had a lot of strength of character. When he didn't want to drink he wouldn't for a long time," recalls another friend. "Even when he drank too much he might have been belligerent, but his mind still worked. But what would happen is his face would get very red and livid. Until near the end it wasn't an ongoing thing, just a sometime thing."[51]

For some people this "sometime thing" can be the dominant force in their ability to adapt and deal with the problem. For some it's the prime thing. No matter how great a person's intelligence, it provides no protection against alcohol. A company executive always used to being in control and getting his own way, who suddenly finds himself in a situation he can't control can be devastated. Alcohol can do that to people, destroy their ability to control their craving. They are unable to accept the fact that what they have is an incurable disease. Their bodies usually adapt and over a period of time they cannot function without alcohol. Such was what was happening to Gordon. The "sometime thing" was gradually becoming the "most of the time thing".

But despite the alcohol, Audrey "always thought it was a great love affair and it was. They had a lot of fun together; they communicated well but it was difficult for her. She worried about Crawford an awful lot. She used to get very angry with him, the air would be blue in the office sometimes, but she could always hold her own with him. All she was looking for was peace."[52]

When Gordon was in Halifax attending Guest's funeral, Audrey decided to leave. "Her family wanted to take a holiday," recalls a friend, "and they wanted to drive to California, so she decided that she would get away from this; it had become an impossible situation for her, so she left. She finally got him out of her system but I don't think he really ever got her out of his."[53]

This would prove truer than both Audrey and Crawford realized.

A.V. ROE CANADA TAKES OFF

"Today," aviation reporter Jim Hornick wrote in *The Globe and Mail* in February 1953 because of the coming of Crawford Gordon to A.V. Roe, "the aircraft assembly lines are filled with aircraft. All the difficulties have not yet been solved, but Avro has battled its way into the front rank of the jet producers, confident that what lies ahead will be trivial when compared to what lies behind."[54] Maybe so, but 1954 began with Crawford Gordon getting himself a new airplane and a new secretary.

On the first day of the year, C.D. Howe reluctantly announced that his department had issued a design contract to Avro Aircraft to construct a prototype for an advanced jet aircraft he had designated the CF-105, citing that, "for a comparatively modest expenditure to produce a prototype is cheap defence insurance." He went on to describe the revolutionary aspects of the aircraft, saying it would weigh over 30 tons, fly at speeds of 1,200 mph, have a range of 1500 miles and probably fire guided missiles.[55] Although he refused to let the company build the C-102 Jetliner, he was now prepared to let them build the CF-105 Avro Arrow.

"Because of the tremendous urgency of the Arrow program," writes Jim Floyd, "it was decided to eliminate the building of prototype aircraft and virtually go straight into production with 'hard tooling' on the first aircraft. Only those who have been associated with the design of new aircraft will even begin to appreciate the tremendous pressures put onto engineering by the combination of these decisions."[56] And because the Rolls Royce RB-106 was not available, the company was building a new engine as well. "We think," said Gordon, "it is the most advanced jet engine in the world. We expect it will reach 20,000 lbs static thrust, at least three times more powerful than our Orenda, and we expect the engine will be used in our new delta-winged aircraft."[57]

"Here we were," writes Jim Floyd, "dealing with an aircraft more complex in every way than any previous service project, and there were few reports or tests to substantiate the design features. We also had a brand new engine to develop at the same time (a combination avoided if at all possible by every aircraft designer since Icarus), and we were to issue full production drawings from scratch, from which permanent hard tools were made, well prior to even the basic testing program being completed."[58]

* * * *

In the summer of 1954, being Crawford Gordon's secretary was described as "the top female job in Canada."[59] And Gloria Collinson, who would end up in that role longer than any other, describes how that transpired:

I had recently separated and went to live with my father and mother in Oakville, recalls Collinson, and I couldn't quite figure out what I was going to do until my father, who worked at Avro, saw an ad in the paper asking for a personal assistant to Crawford Gordon. They interviewed about 200 people and I had six interviews when I learned that Crawford had seen six or seven girls, was quite rude to them and turned them all down.

When I finally met him he took a look at me, asked a few questions then said: 'Well I think that's fine' and walked out of the interview. After he left, the interviewers said: 'Well that looks pretty good' and the next week I was offered the job.

At the end of my second week there, Crawford said I should get a car to get to work and when I told him I rented a car, he couldn't believe it and arranged for someone to pick me up every day until I bought an old clunker to get me to work.

I was fully aware that I had replaced Audrey Underwood. I immediately knew the Audrey Underwood story. He did pursue her long after she wanted to be pursued, and she would always give in. She would always tell me: 'I'll never see him again!' but she always did. He was a very strong personality.[60]

* * * *

On June 6, 1953 retired Air Marshall Wilf Curtis joined the board of directors of A.V. Roe Canada as vice-chairman, succeeding Canadian millionaire J.P. Bicker who had passed away some months earlier. Sir Roy Dobson still retained the chairmanship, albeit from across the ocean in England. Wilfred Austin Curtis, both likeable and popular, was in many people's eyes the father of the modern RCAF. Born in the village of Havelock, Ontario in 1893, Curtis had been a Canadian army officer in the First World War before joining the Royal Naval Air Service in Britain. He was credited with shooting down 13 enemy aircraft and awarded the Distinguished Service Cross and Bar before returning to Toronto to found and operate the W.A. Curtis Insurance Company. In 1932 he rejoined the RCAF, but it was his Second World War experience in the allocation of Canadian-made aircraft to other countries that made him an advocate of an air force flying Canadian-designed and -built aircraft.

Curtis had played an intimate role with the development of the CF-100 and it only seemed natural he would be suitably rewarded with a position on the board of the company that got the contract to build nearly 700 of them. "He really didn't have any authority in the company," recalls Fred Smye, "but he thought it would be an opportunity to continue to support the air force in its independence. And we always relied on his experience."[61] Curtis received an annual retainer of $20,000, a limousine and a chauffeur.

* * * *

In April, Pat Kelly's public relations campaign began to show its influence on Crawford Gordon. In an interview to *The Globe and Mail*, Gordon talked about the value and importance he put on hiring disabled individuals as employees. That was quite a step for a corporation in 1954. Boasting that the company had over 300 handicapped people in its employ including six blind people, Gordon would say: "Employing handicapped persons can be good business for the company concerned and the community at large. We're glad to have them."[62] And a week later he would take another unorthodox step for the time when he unilaterally cancelled the company's annual golf tournament at the Lakeview Golf Club in Toronto because they refused admission to one of the company's employees because of his colour.

* * * *

Gordon's company continued to expand at a rapid pace. New versions of the CF-100 went into production — Mark 3 through 5 — and Avro also won the overhaul contracts. The government had issued development contracts for the new CF-105 fighter and the new engine to power it. Still sensitive to the delays experienced in getting the CF-100 into production, the company was hampered by its dependence on over 400 subcontractors for everything from metals, plastics and electronics to rubber and alloys. During the war C.D. Howe had taught Gordon a basic principle of production — control your source of supply — and on December 4, 1954, Gordon moved to do just that. He took the first step in enlarging the A.V. Roe Canada family by buying Canadian Steel Improvement (CSI).

"When you have a company that's built solely on government contracts," says Crawford Gordon III, "there's a certain amount of political interference. You're highly dependent on that one agency — the government. I mean it's only sensible to diversify if you can. Rothman's, for instance, diversified out of tobacco because if everyone gave up smoking, Rothman's would be finished. So you diversify and that's what he did."[63]

The purchase made sense since CSI was a Hawker-Siddeley subsidiary which supplied jet blades for the Orenda engines. In keeping with his concept of how a company should operate, subsidiary or not, CSI would continue to have its own board of directors, finance, legal, industrial relations and public relations sections with policy and overall coordination coming from the parent, A.V. Roe Canada.

"These changes may be likened to the coming of age of members of a family," Gordon would say on the acquisition, "wherein each has attained his majority and is capable of carrying out his own destiny without in any way ceasing to be part of the family."[64] And as 1954 came to an end, Gordon was poised to expand his family beyond aircraft and engines — into shipping, steel products, trucks and buses, iron ore, coal, railway rolling stock, computers and electronics.

By early 1955, the company's employment offices were receiving over 2,000 inquiries per month, with industrial relations and personnel department staff travelling more that 25,000 miles per year in the search of desperately needed skilled engineers. Ads were placed in newspapers, magazines, professional journals and even university newspapers. The company went as far as to host and pay for a conference with the 30,000-strong Dominion Council of Professional Engineers to look at what Gordon perceived as the shortage of scientific and engineering expertise in Canada.

The situation is so bad, Gordon would say in a speech prepared by Pat Kelly for the conference, I'm reminded of the story in Business Week *recently about the man who was recruiting engineers for his company. He had taken a hotel suite and while interviewing a particularly good prospect, the switchboard called to say the hotel was on fire and for everybody to pass the alarm along and get out. As calmly as he could, the recruiting officer hung up, finished the interview, and only after the prospect had been safely signed, did he yell 'fire.'*

This isn't as far fetched as it may seem. I was reading the other day where an official of the Atomic Energy plant was touring universities in Western Canada to interview this year's graduates. He found as many as 80 United States firms had been ahead of him and in some cases, offered jobs to the entire class.

We've had United States companies 'raid' us. They've offered our people all-expense-paid trips to as far away as California just to see their facilities and surroundings and, of course, climate. In some cases those who went were moved bag and baggage, free of charge. Homes were found for them as well.

I don't propose to go into details of the future. We're talking about a Canada in 1980 with probably twice as many people, producing three times as much as today, earning 50 per cent more for a much shorter week and enjoying the highest standard of living in the world.

But in almost every case, this truly inspiring panoramic projection of Canada tomorrow was hedged with a big if. All this

*can come true if we can produce the men and women intel-
lectually trained to bring it about. This is the bottleneck today
and unless we do something to correct it, it will be an even
worse bottleneck in the future.*[65]

In another speech authored by Pat Kelly for the Canada Club in
Toronto in early March, Gordon referred to the Arrow under development at Malton.

*It is common knowledge too that the interceptor of tomorrow
— maybe we should have it today — will have to fly at Mach
2 or 1,520 mph at sea level. But whether we will see the day
when an atomic-powered aircraft will be able to fly around
the earth on a few pounds of fuel remains to be seen. It is by
no means impossible that this could happen in our lifetime.*

*No matter what the cost, we must somehow find the money
because continuing and unremitting research and development is the key to survival.*

*I think our experience to date shows that it hasn't cost any
more to design the CF-100 and the Orenda engine than it
would have cost to buy a licence to build someone else's plane
and engine and, on top of that, pay a royalty on every one
produced.*[66]

This may have been true in 1956 terms but certainly not by the time
the Arrow took flight two years later.

* * * *

Joining a rapidly growing company like A.V. Roe Canada in 1955
must have been a great adventure for young professionals. A new
employee would immediately be required to take an oath of secrecy
to reveal to no one any and all matters concerning the production of
aircraft or engines. Employees were issued a company photo ID with
a coloured dot indicating which of the four levels of security access
they had. Security was crucial at the Malton plant, and the company's

security force was larger than that in many small towns in Canada. All the company's security guards were sworn constables of the Peel County Police and were frequently called for duty outside the plant gates. They patrolled over 600 miles a week within the plant and directed over 5,000 cars in and out of the parking lots every day. In fact, at the time, Avro had the dubious distinction of creating the worst traffic jams in the whole country.

Upon joining, a new employee was entitled to a company-paid group insurance plan, a pension plan, transportation, housing, recreation, food services and employee counselling. A computer matched available and needed rides to work to a map of any location within 80 miles of the plant. Employee Services kept an ongoing list of over 200 houses, apartments, flats and rooms, furnished or unfurnished, for immediate occupancy until the new employee found something more permanent. And the company found itself in the housing business, building over 1,000 homes for its employees at locations in western Toronto. These were available for purchase for a mere ten per cent down payment.

A full-time recreation supervisor and the Recreation Club Committee assisted in organizing and directing some 30 clubs and activities. Members contributed 25 cents per month through payroll deduction, which was matched by the company. Activities included basketball, skiing, bowling, hockey, tennis, softball, golf, badminton and hobbies such as photography and model-aircraft building. For many, the company was nicknamed "cupid's paradise," with men outnumbering women by 13 to 1.

The Avro Choir and the Avro-Orenda Pipe Band performed free for charity and community functions. Dances, annual Christmas parties and summer picnics for employees and their families were arranged and were very popular. Food Services was responsible for running the cafeterias and the executive dining room. Because the company ran three shifts around the clock, lunches and dinners were prepared at a central commissary and delivered by mobile units to various "feeding stations" throughout the plants. As well, many employees benefited from employee counselling which was equipped to deal with personal, business or educational matters. The plant had its own hospital, staffed by a medical director and nurses, which treated over 63,000 injuries in 1955 alone. In addition, the company made frequent donations to local hospitals. Humber Memorial Hospital received $25,000 in 1955 and the Malton District Hospital received $32,000 towards their building fund in 1956.

Company inventory included over 11,000 pieces of furniture, not including over 1,000 typewriters, calculators and adding machines. The archives housed over 82 tons of company records dating back to 1945. The mail room handled over 12,000 pieces of internal and external mail every working day, and the company telephone exchange sat on 83 trunk lines, handling 1,629 telephones.

* * * *

For its tenth anniversary in 1955, A.V. Roe Canada decided to throw itself a birthday party. It was held at the King Edward Hotel in Toronto on December 1 and to commemorate the occasion, the company gave out Avro and Orenda ten-year pins. All the management committee and board of directors were there (among them company founder Sir Roy Dobson), as well as an audience of 300, including 19 women. Although present for the ceremonies, Crawford Gordon did not get a pin, having only been with the company for four years — since 1951.

"I really had hoped six years from now to get one of these pins after having won my spurs," Gordon said. "Because without the complete and utter support of everybody here, I would be completely useless."[67] Gordon then introduced Sir Roy Dobson. "Now, it has always been a matter of some doubt to me as to how you define a Canadian," Gordon began. "I prefer to think of a Canadian as one who believes in Canada, and who works hard at it. And on this score, I suggest to you that no one qualifies any better that Sir Roy Dobson."[68]

Dobson reflected on his first trip to Canada in 1943 and how the company had come into being. He talked about his relationship with C.D. Howe but he saved most of his praise for Gordon.

In 1951 I felt the company needed strengthening all over including top management, he would say, where Fred Smye was 'worked to a frazzle' and Walter Deischer [the first president] 'a sick man.' I had heard earlier about Crawford Gordon in Canadian industry and said that the day he came to A.V. Roe Canada would be the very big turning point in the history of our company. Not only did I hire that day a most successful young president and general manager, I made a friend, one of the best friends I ever had. And I don't want any better ... When he sets his mind to do a job, he'll do it in spite of hell and high water. And that is what he has done in A. V. Roe. If you compare A. V. Roe now to what it was just over four short years ago when Crawford came, you will realize some of the things he has done. You can rely on him. As long as he is at the helm of this company, you haven't anything to worry about.

What about the future, boys? Well, aircraft and engines are going higher and farther and faster... You will get into electronic things ... You will get into missiles. You cannot avoid it. All kinds of fine engineering will have to be developed within our Group ... Maybe the future will have some fancy gas turbine or diesel trains too. Those things have got to come.... [69]

And come they did. Gordon was once again eager to add to the A.V. Roe family. Offering $30 a share, Gordon acquired his second company, Canadian Car and Foundry, with divisions in Montreal and Fort William. The company produced freight and passenger railway equipment as well as metal castings; their Montreal operation was one of the largest foundries in Canada. The automotive and aircraft divisions in Fort William produced buses, transport trailers and military aircraft and components. Canadian Car and Foundry had assets totaling $36 million; Gordon got the entire operation for $21 million. However, soon after the acquisition, Gordon divided the company in two: Canadian Car and Foundry and Canadian Steel Foundries. He then spent an additional $19 million to modernize and expand both operations. Gordon's acquisition of Canadian Car and Foundry was another attempt at securing his sources of supply.

"Ironically," writes author Jim Dow, "the Hurricane [fighters] that Wilf Curtis tried unsuccessfully to get during the war had been produced at the Fort William plant. To the new vice-chairman of the board of A.V. Roe, this part of the acquisition must have been particularly sweet."[70]

"We did it," said Gordon later, "to broaden our industrial base and diversify operations and interests. With one stride," he boasted, "we, as a country and company, stepped into what is unquestionably one of the toughest design and manufacturing businesses in the world. And despite our late start, we're doing all right."[71]

And how did Gordon's mentor C.D. Howe react to the purchase? He admitted that he was "surprised" when he heard of the deal, and snapped that he, "did not like companies that are too big but Can-Car is not a major aircraft company."[72] But if it had been, would that have made a difference?

* * * *

As 1955 rolled into 1956, and with two new corporations operating under A.V. Roe Canada, Crawford Gordon felt his company had to have a motto, an inspirational saying much like GM's: "What's Good for General Motors Is Good for America." Gordon originally wanted to use the saying for which he was known from his McGill days: "Let's Go!" But Pat Kelly thought that was too brash. His suggestion, "The Next Big Step," had more impact and implied a strong future. So in January 1965, "The Next Big Step" became the company motto of A.V. Roe Canada.

* * * *

By 1956, Gordon was experiencing what most company executives go through, spending more and more time in the office and less and less time at home. And he had less and less time for frivolities. "I'd be there at my desk first thing in the morning," recalls former secretary Gloria Collinson. "And he had a big office and the door would suddenly open and he would stride through, tall and arms ever so straight. Sometimes he'd say hello; sometimes he wouldn't. And the next thing you know the buzzer on my desk would go and another long day would start."[73]

By this time Gordon's former secretary Audrey Underwood had tried to make a new life for herself after leaving behind Crawford Gordon and A.V. Roe, but it wasn't easy. She lived in California for a time, then moved to New York. Getting employment was easy for her since she had worked for one of the most senior executives in one of the largest companies in Canada. It had been hard on Crawford to let her go. In fact, he never really did let her go. He always kept track of where she was and, on more than one occasion, showed up at her door in the wee hours of the morning, totally drunk. Even though Audrey got sick of it after a while, she would tell friends she didn't have the heart to turn him away. But Gordon's periodic absences were starting to be felt at Malton.

"I knew he'd tracked her down and looked her up. I knew it," recalls a former executive secretary. "I once cornered him at a company social and said, 'If you think for one minute I don't know what you don't want me to know, you think again.' He just looked at me and raised his eyebrows and said: 'I just love that little guy' [his pet name for Audrey]."[74]

And yet, despite his chasing after Audrey, Gordon remained "very much in love with Mary," recalls Gloria Collinson. "I remember the Christmas he bought Mary a car. He had it tied up in a big ribbon and put in the driveway of their home, and he was like a kid for weeks before she got it because he was so anxious for her to see it."[75]

Sir Roy Dobson was becoming concerned with the dalliance and drinking of his young president. Yet his concern was more out of regard for the man than for the office he represented. As time went by, Dobson more and more had come to see Crawford Gordon as a son. And Gordon was more than happy to reciprocate. By 1956 A.V. Roe Canada was quickly becoming the most profitable part of the Hawker-Siddeley Group. Tom Sopwith, Hawker-Siddeley's chairman, after whom the famous First World War fighter was named, wanted to retire and Dobson was desperate to secure the managing director's position. Legend has it he called Gordon for help and Gordon secured the resignations of all A.V. Roe Canada executives and board members and threatened to offer them up if Dobson didn't get the position. Dobson got the position.

A.V. ROE CANADA GOES PUBLIC

Gordon's acquisition of Canadian Steel Improvement and Canadian Car and Foundry generated some ripples of concern within the Canadian economic community. 1956 was the year Walter Gordon, the Canadian economic nationalist, had chaired the Royal Commission on Canada's Economic Prospects which drew attention to foreign ownership in Canada and the notion of economic nationalism.

Many Canadians, writes Jim Dow, "were becoming increasingly concerned about the changing character of foreign investment ... Through reinvestment of earnings, a subsidiary was able to grow, either by improving its own facilities or simply by buying out other firms, in a process that was effectively closed to Canadian investors. When A. V. Roe began to diversify in 1955, it was to a great extent like buying us out with our own money."[76]

"This company is as Canadian as it could well be," Sir Roy Dobson said. "We have brought key designers and engineers here who, in most cases, are staying here and becoming Canadian. We have made it our policy to buy materials or parts in Canada. Our buying is Canadian and our employment is Canadian."[77]

In response to what A. V. Roe was trying to do, Crawford Gordon took his own particular brand of Canadian nationalism to the prestigious Canadian Club in New York City on May 24. Calling Americans "selfish" and "narrow" and while admitting that American capital was heartily welcome in Canada, he stated that, "Canadians feel that too often the investment has taken the form of American-managed branch operation. There is a massive ignorance of Canada by a vast number of Americans."[78]

And later, upon receiving an honorary degree from St. Francis Xavier University in Antigonish, Nova Scotia, he said, "It has been easier to import ideas, plans and money from our American friends rather than provide these ourselves. But in all this assistance, there is a good measure of hazard."[79]

Despite Gordon's nationalistic overtones, by the fall, critics of the company still labelled A.V. Roe as a British, and therefore foreign, corporation. Gordon, after all, couldn't continue to tell the Americans what to do with their money when Great Britain was telling him what to do with his.

"Our Canadian Group has now become a vital part of the Canadian economy in which every Canadian citizen is interested," former Hawker-Siddeley chairman Tom Sopwith would tell the *Financial Post* in October. "At the same time it has become a matter of concern to the Canadian people that so much of their industrial activity is in the hands of non-resident owners and, whilst they welcome the assistance which is being given in developing their vast potential resources, there is a growing feeling that they should be allowed to share in the ownership, as well as the operation of these activities."[80] Gordon knew that if A. V. Roe Canada was going to acquire any more companies and expand, it wouldn't be able to do it on the "cost plus 5 per cent" of his government contracts for aircraft and engines. It was time to go public as a corporation.

Wood Gundy was perhaps the best-known financial firm on Bay Street in Toronto at the time and Gordon knew Pete Scott, the firm's chairman and Charles Gundy, one of the firm's principles. With board approval, Gordon approached Wood Gundy to see if they'd be willing to underwrite the selling of shares. He presented them with a five-year history of A. V. Roe, allowing Wood Gundy to determine whether Canadians would buy shares in the company, how much money could be raised and what the selling price per share would be. The time, they determined, was just right.

"Wood Gundy tapped the market when the psychology was right," says Crawford Gordon III. "And that provided my father with enough money for the piggy bank."[81]

"Since the inception of A. V. Roe Canada Ltd. in 1945," read Wood Gundy's prospectus, "it has been the intention of the parent company, Hawker-Siddeley Group Ltd., to afford an opportunity to the Canadian public to invest in the company at a proper stage in the development of its business. After ten years of growth and reinvestment of earnings, it is considered that this stage has been reached."[82] That stage involved an $8 million offering of some 500,000 common shares of A. V. Roe Canada stock at $16 per share. This would allow Canadians to acquire 17 per cent of the company. Sixteen dollars per share for A.V. Roe stock in 1956 was considered to be an offering of what financial people call blue chip stock. The company went public because it showed a reasonable success over a five-year period and because Gordon needed the capital to acquire more subsidiaries. His mantra, as always, was: control your source of supply.

"When A. V. Roe went public," recalls Pat Kelly, "Gordon phoned me at home one night and said, 'I'm making out my "special" list, so how many shares do you want?' I said that 500 would be just fine and he said, 'Oh, I'll put you down for 10,000.' And I said, 'I can't do that. I can't afford it.' 'Well put a mortgage on your house,' he said, and I told him I couldn't do it, I was not that type, so I took 500 shares but courtesy of the Royal Bank."[83]

Gordon now had $8 million from the shares issued and he wasted no time in deciding what to do with it. John Tory, the company's legal advisor, had just returned from Montreal and a visit with his friend C.B. Lang who was ill. Lang had told Tory how much he admired A. V. Roe and that his own company was for sale. Tory told Gordon about the conversation, and Gordon realized that the company for sale was the same one he had heard about when he was in Nova Scotia three years before: the iron ore company — Dosco.

A.V. ROE CANADA SOARS

Without a doubt, 1957 was A. V. Roe Canada's and, in many ways Crawford Gordon's, best year. It was a year of wins and losses but the wins, for the last time in his life, outnumbered the losses. That year would be the year Gordon's company would take "the next big steps" and blossom into a complex of 44 companies with 50,000 employees. A. V. Roe Canada would find their name on the list of the top 100 companies in the world, the top 80 companies in North America and the top three in Canada, behind only the CPR and Alcan.

"I think that our company has demonstrated that we belong in the realm of exciting projects," Gordon would write in an article to his employees. "We're going to stay there. We have plans for the future, and we have expansion programs under way to back up those plans. We have the design, engineering and research facilities to keep up with the pack or stay a bit ahead. We've shown that we can produce as efficiently as anyone. And, we have the right kind of people. In the final analysis, that counts for more than anything else. To me, our future is unlimited."[84]

The year began with the company losing one aircraft and gaining another. Calling the C-102 Jetliner "a casualty of the Korean War,"[85] the plane was ordered grounded and cut up for scrap after a nearly flawless flight-test record lasting eight years. On the other hand, the company's new aircraft, the CF-105, was now given the name "Arrow" because of its distinctive delta-wing shape.

Nineteen fifty-seven was also the year Canadians would gain 40 per cent control of A. V. Roe. Also the company that had once been entirely dependent on the military and the government for contracts, could now claim that 60 per cent of their business was civilian. It would also be the year they would unveil their revolutionary Arrow aircraft, and the year the country would elect John George Diefenbaker as prime minister of Canada.

Crawford Gordon continued to broaden A. V. Roe's industrial base even further, away from just aircraft and engines. In February he acquired the aerial survey and electronics equipment company, Canadian Applied Research Ltd., and in May A.V. Roe got into steel when Gordon spent $18 million for 11 per cent of the Algoma Steel Corporation.

* * * *

Gordon was gaining the reputation of being very much a loner. There hadn't been much written about him to this point in his career beyond a quote or two in *The Toronto Star* or *The Globe and Mail*. He rarely gave interviews, and the few he did give were strictly about business — what A. V. Roe Canada had done or was about to do. Crawford Gordon was a very private person. In many ways he hadn't changed much from the 17-year-old who walked out of Appleby College 26 years earlier — alone, with few friends and yet determined as hell. He was passionate about the half dozen people he considered close friends. They did any number of things together from attending sporting events, to cottaging, and, of course, drinking long into the night.

He was a company executive unlike any other in that he broke one of the cardinal rules of the business world: he refused to network. To this point in his life, Gordon had gone through three experiences for which company executives would have given their eyeteeth, especially company executives on the way up. He had gone to Appleby College and could have developed some important schoolboy connections; he had gone to McGill University; and most of all, he had been one of Howe's Boys and moreover, his Wonder Boy. And yet, as soon as he was out the door, as soon as he had walked away from any of these network-building opportunities, he never looked back. Crawford Gordon never felt that social cultivation was necessary. He could do it all himself, thank you. He didn't need any help. "He was not a politician and didn't covet friendship," recalls his son Crawford. "He played with friendship. Not in a mean sense, it just wasn't part of his agenda. He was just interested in getting the job done. Who knows, maybe he was still trying to prove something to his parents. Or maybe to himself."[86]

THE DOMINION STEEL AND COAL CORPORATION (DOSCO)

Nowhere was Gordon's loner quality more evident than when he started to expand the A.V. Roe empire, "secure his sources of supply" and acquire corporation after corporation. First he'd read the company's latest annual report, then closet himself in his office at Malton with three people. On his right would be John Tory, the company's legal adviser, on his left would be Pat Kelly, his "Grey Eminence," and in front of him would be his secretary, Gloria Collinson and a telephone. On occasion he might call on some financial people at Wood Gundy, but mostly he was on his own. And then he'd start shuffling and dealing like an old-time Mississippi riverboat gambler. The Dominion Steel and Coal Corporation (Dosco) was a case in point. He impulsively bought the Nova Scotia iron and steel company without doing his homework, and it would prove disastrous. Dosco was only one of many companies Gordon bought on his own, with little consultation and even less caution. But he was where he wanted to be, doing things the way he liked to do things — alone and in control.

"I think he probably started to believe in his own press clippings," recalls his old friend George Mara. "The C.D. Howe romance was such that he felt he had all this power. He had a feeling he wasn't going to display any weakness by asking for advice. He felt he could figure it out himself. I remember one time he returned from a business trip and the company chauffeur drove out with the company car on to the tarmac to meet him. He had words with the chauffeur and ended up driving the car himself. Before long he was stopped by the police and he actually took a swing at the cop that stopped him. He was developing a real arrogance at this time."[87]

The "biggest deal in Canada's industrial history"[88] to that point almost didn't happen. The Dominion Steel and Coal Corporation of Nova Scotia was the third largest steel producer in Canada in 1957. With sales of $210 million and assets of $151 million, Dosco had annual profit of $7 million. And it had just invested $100 million in modernization. Dosco had been incorporated in 1928 as part of the reorganization of the British Empire Steel Corporation. Over the years it had become a fully integrated operation, including mining and advanced metal fabrication. Its products included iron ore, coal, coke, pig-iron, ingots, forgings, bars, nails, ships, railroad rolling stock and iron bridges. It was comprised of 55 subsidiaries including Dominion Iron and Steel, Dominion Shipping Company, Halifax Shipyards Ltd., Dominion Wabana Ore, Canadian Bridge Company, Canadian Tube and Steel Products and the Dominion Coal Company. The conglomerate and its subsidiaries employed more than 30,000 people, more than any other single Canadian company.

Pat Kelly fought Gordon over the deal. "Gordon never took the time to read the history of the company," he recalls. "Dosco had only made money during the world wars and was too far from markets. I was against the acquisition; it had been watered down to death by Beaverbrook [too diversified and too spread out in its operation] and so forth. It had originally been a rail factory and it still needed a good deal of modernization. And its company president was dying in hospital in Montreal."[89] Kelly might have been right. The company was indeed distant from the main Canadian market place and recently its coal sales had suffered under the impact of cheaper natural gas. In 1957 Dosco's steel mill production was only running at between 70 per cent and 80 per cent capacity, high by some standards but well below the national average. Its profits for that year were low as well, around $3 million, the lowest in years. But what was hurting the company the most was the reputation it had of being the "sick elephant of the Maritimes."[90]

Stories of Gordon's interest in Dosco had been in the rumour mill of the country's financial community for months. Even during a market slump in the spring of 1957, A. V. Roe's stock had risen from $17 to $25 a share. But Gordon wasn't the only party eyeing Dosco. Phoenix-Rheinrohr and Mannesman International Corp., two German companies, were also interested. When Sir Roy Dobson heard this, he cabled Gordon to get moving on a deal and quickly. "I don't want to see any German interests controlling steel manufacturing in Canada."[91]

"I must have spent at least six full weeks in Gordon's office over the Dosco deal," recalls Pat Kelly. "Gordon had been in Montreal trying to raise the money for the deal. The offer to take over was for cash and stock to the shareholders of Dosco. Gordon was trapped. 'Jesus,' he said to me, 'I'm in an awful jam. I've got to get $4 million right away.' So I sat there with him while he talked to the presidents of banks, and between calls he turns to me and says, 'You've got some Roe stock don't you?' And I said, 'Yes, 500 shares.' And he said: 'What are you going to do with them? Sell them to me.' And I said: 'Nothing doing. I bought them as an investment.'

"So he sold his own stock to raise money for the acquisition. Roe stocks had originally sold for $16 a share; he got them for $10 a share and sold them for $25.50 a share. Fancy that, a man entrusted with running a company selling his own stock."[92]

On August 7 a Montreal newspaper quoted ailing Dosco president C.B. Lang as denying receiving any offer from A. V. Roe for the purchase of Dosco, only a letter of intent. Reactions to Gordon's move to buy Dosco were, according to *Saturday Night* magazine, "swift and sometimes violent."[93] And most of the reaction was from the East Coast.

Dosco's directors were divided. The factions on the board in favour of the sale felt the company needed new cash and efficient management, but others claimed "the deal would take control of Dosco out of Canada because Roe control is held by the Hawker-Siddeley Group of Great Britain. They said Dosco would be dismembered and parts closed down with subsequent unemployment and economic distress for the Maritimes."[94] Dosco director, R.A. Jodrey, called Gordon's offer "ridiculous," claiming the company's Wabano ore reserves alone were worth more than the total Roe offer.[95]

R.J. Bennet, the mayor of New Glasgow, Dosco's home, said Dosco employees and their families were quite alarmed at the Roe offer, adding it was a "pure steal. We're afraid they'll close down Eastern Car [a Dosco subsidiary] … They [Roe] have already spent $15 million on Canadian Car. They won't want Eastern Car too."[96]

To respond to the opposition, Gordon drafted a letter to every Dosco shareholder, stating that A.V. Roe was prepared, "to put up as much as $100 million in shares and cash because we are convinced the Dosco group of companies has tremendous growth and expansion potential. The idea being put forward in some areas, that we only want Dosco to close up part or all of it, is too ill fetched to require a reply."[97]

But the opposition didn't diminish. "How do we know what Roe stock will be worth?" snapped R.A. Jodrey. "The market for it is so thin, and so much of it is held outside Canada, nobody can say what it will be worth. And what does Roe know about the steel business anyway? They have never run anything on a competitive basis. I say Roe's just seen the handwriting on the wall. The aircraft business is on the skids and they just want to save their skins with Dosco."[98] Was this prescience or luck on Jodrey's part? On August 10, 1957 the Dosco board approved the deal and Gordon took a 77 per cent control of the company and brought it — reluctantly — into the A. V. Roe family. Gordon assumed the presidency of Dosco as well as his A.V. Roe duties.

Soon after taking over Dosco, Gordon learned another lesson about doing business in Quebec reminiscent of his days with CGE in Schenectady. Faced with an impending strike in Dosco's Montreal operation, he put a call into Premier Maurice Duplessis. The two men had met previously and liked each other. Gordon told the premier of the impending strike and asked him for help.

"Well I don't know about the strike Monsieur Gordon," said the Premier, "but while I have you on the phone, I think you might invite my friend Monsieur Jean Raymond to join your board of directors." Raymond was a bagman for the Union Nationale at the time.

"But of course," replied Gordon. "It would be a pleasure to do just that." End of conversation. End of impending strike.[99]

"Avro is now in the three basic areas we set out to get into," Gordon said on the takeover. "Defence, transportation and steel. We've come a long way and we're going a lot further — a whole lot further. To me, the future is unlimited."[100] And so it seemed.

DIEF AND THE AVRO ARROW

The House of Commons was made aware that between January 1, 1949 and February 28, 1957, the Department of National Defence had paid out a total of $967,371,827 to A. V. Roe Canada for a number of overhaul and development aircraft contracts. This did not include payments on the engine development contracts with the Chinook, Orenda and Iroquois. The company's policy of operating at "cost plus 5 per cent" had made A. V. Roe a profit of close to $50 million on just the aircraft development contracts. Of this amount, over $99 million had been spent on the Arrow program alone.

C.D. Howe now visited the Malton plant less and less frequently. There really was no need to since the CF-100 program was in full production and Canada's air squadrons were being equipped on an almost monthly basis. Howe and Gordon still talked on the phone occasionally but not as often as they had during Gordon's first months with A.V. Roe. Nonetheless, the minister still remained troubled about one thing — the Avro Arrow.

"We have embarked on a program of development which gives me the shudders," he had revealed in the House in June 1955, "a supersonic plane and a supersonic engine." Privately, he would tell friends that the Arrow program "disturbed his sleep." But the Arrow program was a Liberal program, and if things really got out of hand, Howe could cancel it just like he had threatened to do with the CF-100. And there would be plenty of time for that — at least another four more years.

Louis St. Laurent had called a general election for June of 1957 and the Liberals fully expected to be returned to office, despite the fact that the Conservative Party had elected a new leader in the person of John Diefenbaker, an old adversary of Howe's. The polls in January indicated the Liberals were leading the Conservatives by 48 per cent to 31 per cent in popularity. It looked as if Howe would, indeed, have plenty of time to look at the Arrow program.

However, Canadian voters were looking for change. They were tired of Liberal arrogance, typified by the infamous Pipeline Debate in which C.D. Howe pushed through the controversial TransCanada Pipeline by invoking closure, and cutting off debate in the House of Commons. But the debate went on in the streets and living rooms of Canada. On election night, June 10, 1957, the country's voters returned a Conservative government, a minority, the first since the 1930s. Even C.D. Howe lost his seat and after more than two decades of Liberal rule, John George Diefenbaker found himself Prime Minister of Canada.

Although born in Ontario, Diefenbaker had deep affections and close ties to Saskatchewan. He was known as a small-time Prairie lawyer and while he might have had some knowledge of freight rates, wheat tariffs and hog prices, his knowledge of aircraft, to say nothing of high technology aircraft, was non-existent. And it was this, more than anything, that rankled the executives at A.V. Roe.

When it came to aircraft, writes aviation writer, Bill Gunstone:

> *Dief neither knew nor cared much about semi-active guidance and air-cooled turbine blading. He had swept into office on a tide of electoral promises, most of which were aimed at his homeland where you can fly a light plane over rolling golden wheat for an hour and still not reach the edge of the field. How could Dief make good on his battle-cry that his administration would give the farmers more dough? There seemed to be only one simple way and that was to cancel a major existing project. Long before he came to office, the Arrow had been standing out like a sore thumb. Dief had spent a lot of time from 1955 trying to find out how vital it was to the RCAF. The fairly sudden emergence of the missile as a sort of 'replacement' was a manna from heaven, and when Britain's Duncan Sandys published his Defence White Paper in April 1957, Dief's joy knew no bounds. All he needed now was for something to go sour in the Arrow program.*[101]

> *But who in 1957-58 was prepared to stick his neck out and assert that the manned fighter was NOT finished? Nobody could do it and then slip away quietly. Such an opinion would have meant a thundering argument, and most of the people Dief talked to had careers to think of. I suspect that, whatever the chaps may have believed deep down, almost everyone took the easy way out and sided with the majority which said 'Manned fighters seem to be on the way out. The Arrow is a terribly costly program. It looks as if we'd be better off buying some missiles.' This is what Dief wanted to hear.*[102]

SPUTNIK

Pat Kelly and Crawford Gordon had had a pretty good run of success in turning around the public image of A. V. Roe Canada in the mid-

1950s. Their success was measured in grabbing headlines and the bigger the headline, the bigger the smile on Gordon's face. So successful were they that between the summer of 1957 and February 1959, not a single day went by without at least one story on A.V. Roe in at least one of the three Toronto dailies. And no day was supposed to bring greater headlines than the day they rolled out the Arrow on October 4, 1957.

It was a typical A.V. Roe-organized event, complete with the appropriate VIPs, music, and speeches boasting of past accomplishment and future hopes. A podium crowded with dignitaries positioned in front of the assembly bay in which the Arrow waited, held J.A.D. McCurdy, the famous Canadian aviation pioneer, and no less than two Air Marshalls, four Air Vice Marshalls, two Cabinet ministers, two assistant deputy ministers, three senior USAF people, some MPs, assorted company executives and, of course, Sir Roy Dobson, Fred Smye and Crawford Gordon. Press photos of the event show an uncomfortable Crawford Gordon on the podium that day, in dark suit and fedora behind dark sunglasses. He clearly looked out of place at an event that was supposed to put his company on the world stage. In the audience beyond the podium were Gordon's wife Mary and their 19-year-old son, Crawford III. Mary and Crawford were the only two family members attending the roll-out that day. Cynthia and Diana were at Compton School in Quebec and couldn't get away. Compton was Gordon's school of choice mostly because of his desire to have his girls exposed to French, but also because of his love of Montreal and Quebec.

The ceremony was to begin at 2:00 p.m. to allow the press guys to file their stories and meet the evening deadlines for the most widely read Toronto editions of *The Star*, *The Globe* and *The Tely*. When the ceremony was over Gordon, Dobson and Smye returned to Briarcrest for drinks and to eagerly await delivery of the newspapers. The three men took wagers on just how big the type size of the headlines would be. When the papers finally arrived, however, instead of the word Arrow splashed across the front pages, they found the word "SPUTNIK." What was supposed to have been the greatest day in the history of the company and perhaps even the country, the Arrow Unveiling Day was lost, destroyed by Canada's former ally. October

4, 1957 was the day the Russians had chosen to launch the world's first man-made satellite, stealing the Arrow's thunder, in more ways than one, as it turned out. The missile age had arrived.

THE BEGINNING OF THE END

By the end of 1957, Gordon was starting to feel the pressure of running both A.V. Roe Canada and Dosco. The regular trips back and forth between Malton and Halifax and the punishing workload were taking their toll. He had given up most of his recreations — his tennis and his golf — and he was drinking more, sometimes going off for days at a time and spending much too much time at the company estate, Briarcrest. Adding to the business pressures was the death of his father, Crawford Sr., at age 76, while vacationing in Prince Edward Island in August. Gordon was terribly hurt and disappointed when he learned his father had left his entire estate to his younger brother Bill. It wasn't that he needed the money as his less successful brother certainly did. But he would have liked some acknowledgment. In many ways it was Appleby College all over again.

But his father's passing brought an unusual reponse from the most unlikely of people: fatherly interest from Sir Roy Dobson. When Crawford had first joined A.V. Roe Canada in 1951, Dobson hadn't been that keen on the idea since Gordon had been "rough as hell" on his new company over the CF-100 while still at Defence Production in Ottawa. Over the years, however, for Dobson at least, the relationship had deepened to the point where the old man had started to look upon the much younger Gordon more as a son than as an employee. Company insiders who knew Dobson well said it had to do with the loss of his son Jack some 11 years before. Jack Dobson had been one of the first of Dobbie's "special apprentices" at Avro Manchester and had attended the Manchester College of Technology. To those who knew him, he was bright, with a great sense of humour, many friends and no overpowering sense of being the "boss's son." Jack was killed when the BOAC aircraft, in which he was a passenger, disappeared without a trace over the Pacific on March 24, 1946. The aircraft had been on a flight to Australia where Jack was to organize the production of the Avro Lincoln Bomber for the Australian government in Victoria. No sign of the wreckage was ever found. Dobson had hoped that Jack would succeed him as managing director of the Hawker-Siddeley Group and never got over the loss of both a son and potential successor.[103] What Gordon was doing with A. V. Roe Canada, Dobson had hoped that Jack would have done with Hawker-Siddeley. Within two short years, however, the "father" would disown the "son."

* * * *

The year ended on a high note for A. V. Roe and for Crawford Gordon. Although just shy of his forty-fourth birthday, he'd seen his salary rise from $35,000 in 1951 to $75,000 in six years. He now made as much as the President of the United States. Pat Kelly's efforts with the media were working as well. In an article in *Business Week* under the title, "Young Company On The Way Up," Toronto journalist John Harbron put together the most favourable article to date on the corporation and its young president.

> *In 12 short years, wrote Harbron, Avro has grown from a fledgling aircraft maker into Canada's number-three corporation. As recently as two years ago, Avro was a one-product aircraft company dependent on defence business. Today, it is a complex of 44 companies with 50,000 employees and sales in the $450 million-a-year range. And Dobson and Gordon intend to make it the biggest factor in Canadian business.*
>
> *Gordon — who became president in 1951 — had a sharp eye for bargains, a dread of depending on just one customer and no evident worries about his ability to run a vast complex empire. But 1957 has been the year for Avro's most spectacular acquisitions. Management needs time and talent to overcome some of the present problems. First of all top management is spread a little thin. Gordon now has two jobs — the presidency of Dosco, as well as his present duties. [The company] has consciously acquired companies that have been relatively slow of foot. It will take plenty of management time and patience to get them moving again.[104]*

But, by the end of 1957, "plenty of management time and patience" was at a premium — especially for Crawford Gordon.

THE UNCERTAIN FUTURE

Where 1957 had been the company's best year, 1958 would prove to be its most crucial. The formal Arrow roll-out on October 4 was overshadowed and upstaged by a little Soviet satellite called Sputnik. It was the world's first launched satellite, and it knocked the Arrow out of the headlines and eventually out of the sky. And for the first time Canada's defence planners started to think that the day of the piloted interceptor to defend North America was over. Prior to 1957, it was clear that if the Soviets were to attack, they would do so with armed bombers, taking the shortest route over the polar ice cap. The obvious response was the piloted interceptor. Now, with this new missile technology, how useful were manned interceptors? And was the only way to stop a missile with another missile?

Because of Sputnik, wrote Professor James Eayrs, "the intelligence community had forecast that by 1961-2, the major threat to the continent would be missile forces; bombers would be relegated to a secondary role. If such an assessment was correct, it would be difficult to justify such large anti-bomber defence costs, as the forecast threat could be met by other available means at a generally reduced cost." [105]

General Guy Simonds, the former head of the country's Chiefs of Staff Committee, commented that he believed the Arrow, "to be obsolete as a defence weapon, because before it becomes operational, the airplane will have ceased to be the primary weapon of air power." [106] Dr. O.M. Solandt, former chairman of the Defence Research Board, was even blunter. "The Arrow," he commented, "might well be the last piloted airplane to be produced in this country." [107]

But as the debate over whether the manned interceptor was still a viable defence option for Canada on the verge of the missile era continued, the Conservative government, at least in those first months of 1958, were prepared to allow the Arrow and Iroquois programs to continue.

* * * *

At Malton, it was business as usual. On March 25, 1958, the Arrow had its first flight. On its third flight it flew supersonically while climbing and accelerating at 50,000 ft. On the seventh flight it hit 1,000 mph and on subsequent flights it flew to about 1,350 mph. At one point during the test program, pilot Spud Potocki took the Arrow to 1.98 Mach at 3/4 throttle on the J-75 engines, which had 20 per cent less thrust and were heavier than the engine soon to be married to the Arrow: the Iroquois.

> *It seemed to be too good to be true, writes Jim Floyd. And it was. A modern fighter aircraft is really three separate entities. The first is the airplane itself, the second the engine that powers it and the third is the weapons system that arms it. A.V. Roe Canada could control the aircraft and engine side of the plane, but the responsibility and final say in the overall weapons system rested squarely on the RCAF. And they hadn't, as late as 1958, decided on what they wanted.*
>
> *Avro management made no secret of the fact it was most disturbed at the RCAF insistence on specifying the ultimate in fire-control systems — the RCA Astra 1 and a new missile — neither of which were, at the time, even in the design stages — rather than an existing and proven system such as the Hughes MG-3 system with existing Falcon missiles, later to be replaced with the Hughes MX1179 advanced system. From Avro's point of view this added a further risk to the already gigantic task of developing a new aircraft and engine at the same time.*
>
> *The company was apprehensive that development costs of all these items would ultimately be accounted against the aircraft program. This apprehension proved later to be only too correct, since at the time ... the airframe development costs were overshadowed by the anticipated costs of the avionics and armament.*[108]

"That may all be very well," wrote aviation writer Jim Hornick, "but from the point of view of man-hours and money invested, the program will be comparable with the building of the St. Lawrence Seaway."[109] By March, government investment in the Arrow program was in excess of $100 million, not including engine and armament costs. For the first time the Arrow program was threatening to have an impact on the entire defence budget, including those of the army and navy. Some analysts had projected costs to exceed $200 million by the end of the year. By the end of 1958 costs had actually skyrocketed to beyond $350 million.

But in Malton, the company seemed far removed from the debates over costs and missiles and piloted interceptors. On July 5, the annual company picnic drew a record 12,000 employees and their families to a special day at Kiddieland at the CNE grounds. Theatre nights were being organized, houses were still being purchased at a record rate and the company parking lot was filled with many brand-new automobiles.

Dorothy Smye's comment that the company had become more "social" after Gordon's arrival was ringing truer than ever. And nowhere was this more evident that in the antics of Gordon himself. There were stories of his using the company's aircraft to ferry some of his pals to hockey games and boxing matches in cities all across Canada and the United States. Most of the group were not employees, with the exception of maybe Fred Smye, and the converted eight-seater Avro Anson was always full.

One time a bunch of Gordon's pals flew to a heavyweight prizefight in Chicago in December and somebody mentioned that Gordon's birthday was December 26. They decided to buy him a present. The hotel they were staying at was frequented by many high-priced hookers and arrangements were made through the bell captain for one of them to be sent up. She was instructed to go to Gordon's room wearing only a bathrobe and high heels and carrying a birthday cake lit with a single candle. Under the watchful eyes of the guys, she headed down the hall and knocked on Gordon's door. When he was presented with the cake she was pulled into the room with such great force that she almost left her shoes in the hall. She and Gordon didn't surface for several hours.

Even as late as June 1958, company executives seemed oblivious to the defence debates going on in Ottawa over the Arrow program. On June 8 Crawford Gordon invited all the operating heads of the A. V. Roe group of companies to attend a President's Conference at Chantecler, in Ste-Adele, Quebec for the purpose of becoming "better acquainted with each other and each other's operations."[110] The atmosphere was, to say the least, incredibly optimistic.

Walter McLachlan, Gordon's pal from the John Inglis days, and new head of Orenda Engines, spoke first saying he saw A. V. Roe Canada "in terms of the fantastic challenge and opportunity offered by a company that extends all the way from the depths of Nova Scotia coal mines to the outer reaches of space. We have one of the most powerful weapons of the Free World for meeting the competition of Russia and for winning the current struggle for survival."[111]

Archie Baillie, the company's chief financial man, spoke next, saying that the "omnibus accounting Bible" had no place in the corporation and gave a financial snapshot of the company. As of the previous March, A. V. Roe Canada had 1,720 holders of preferred shares and 12,685 holders of common shares. Hawker-Siddeley owned 57 per cent of the company's common capital stock, and 36 per cent of the rest was held in Canada, 6.2 per cent in the United Kingdom (not by Hawker-Siddeley) and the rest in the United States. Bailie also indicated that annual dividend responsibilities to the shareholders amounted to $7.3 million per year.

Ron Williams, head of the company's Public Relations department, spoke next, saying there were many "publics" involved in A. V. Roe's activities including: 45,000 employees, 126,000 dependents of employees, 16,000 shareholders, 6,300 suppliers, 18 municipal governments, seven provincial governments, the armed forces, the federal government and the taxpayers of Canada. It is the function of the Public Relations department, he continued, to interpret the company to the public and to help the company to identify its interests with those of the public.[112]

Next up was Fred Smye who defended the company's history of risking capital on pioneering design and development of aircraft and engines, and said it was the most economical way of equipping the RCAF with both. The operating heads then used the balance of the meeting to deal with day-to-day issues, and the entire assembly was held "spellbound" during a 30-minute presentation on the Arrow and Iroquois programs.[113] They also took time out to play golf, dine together and socialize over drinks. Crawford Gordon adjourned the meeting with the pledge to call the group together on a regular basis.

In fact, A.V. Roe was so confident about its future that it had established a Long Range Planning Committee (LRPC) to look at potential future projects they might undertake. Included was an entire fleet of heavier-than-air vehicles called Pellicans and a scheme for a monorail system to encircle the city of Toronto, nuclear energy projects, anti-ICBM measures, high energy fuels, Electrogravitics, individual flying apparatus and space flight. This group even went as far as to conduct market research on some of these projects and to cost them out as potential contracts.

THE DOWNWARD SPIRAL

With the change in government in Ottawa, A. V. Roe executives lost the luxury of access to information they had when C. D. Howe and the Liberals had been running things. As one would expect, the press was full of stories of the debates going on in Ottawa over the Arrow program, but that's all the information A.V. Roe management had — press reports. The company's Ottawa pipeline had dried up to such a degree that Fred Smye found himself calling Toronto journalists just to get some information. And it was no secret that every member of A. V. Roe Canada's board of directors was Liberal with one exception. John Tory was a long-time bagman for the Conservative Party, but his long association with the company had clouded his ability to get clear, concise information from the office of the prime minister.

The first inkling that there was trouble came from the most unlikely of people in the most unlikely of meetings. In August 1958, Tory had hastily arranged a meeting between Fred Smye and some Conservative Cabinet ministers to "aid in reaching a clear understanding ... as to our future operations."[114] Smye met with Donald Fleming, minister of Finance, Raymond O'Hurley, minister of Defence Production and George Pearkes, minister of Defence.

Smye made a presentation on the Arrow and Iroquois programs, reviewed the entire A. V. Roe operation and made a strong argument that the closing down of those programs would be nothing short of catastrophic. The Cabinet members indicated they were pleased to get the information but Smye, sensing something was not quite right, questioned Finance Minister Donald Fleming.

> *I asked him if a reduction of some $350 million in the Arrow project would make any difference in their considerations, recalls Smye. And he said: 'Mr. Smye, 350 cents would make a difference!' Then Pearkes asked him: 'Suppose we cancel the Arrow, what would you do?'*
>
> *'What would we do?' responded Smye. 'I'd turn the key in the door and walk away.'*
>
> *'Well,' responded Pearkes. 'Can't you build automobiles or something?'[115]*

There were other ominous signs as well. RCAF officers assigned to the Avro plant working on the Arrow program had explicit orders not to discuss the project with company personnel.

But for Crawford Gordon, it seemed his business life couldn't have been better. Now, barely into his forties, Gordon had done just about all he had set out to do: to build one of the largest industrial empires in Canadian history. Everything he had learned on the playing fields of Appleby and McGill or the wartime Ottawa of C.D. Howe had come to this. There's an old saying that when you get it all today, there's nothing left for tomorrow. At 41, Crawford Gordon had nothing left for tomorrow.

Despite his success in business, his personal life was taking a downward spiral. Those who recall seeing Crawford Gordon during the summer of 1958 have a picture in their minds of a man bearing little resemblance to the youthful high-powered executive who took control of A. V. Roe Canada just seven years before. His face was puffier now, much puffier, and his voice, once deep, clear and defiant, now had the tendency to crack at times. And he sometimes left sentences unfinished, as if his mind had trouble finding the right words.

My father was, at 41, at the height of A. V. Roe and dealing with people who were largely 15 years older than himself, recalls Crawford Gordon III. He loved to play golf, squash and tennis and loved watching hockey and football, but when he became so wrapped up in his work he gave them all up. He simply eliminated all his fun things. And, as the stress factors increased, he might have had the physical but not the mental capacity to handle it.

I always thought he was trying to prove something to his parents — this is what drove him — he was always very attentive to his parents, affectionate to my sisters and me but, sadly, never to my mother.[116]

By the summer of 1958 Gordon was seldom home, preferring to spend more and more time at the company estate at Briarcrest, and when he was home, he was usually with Fred Smye, an arm full of papers.

Sometimes his children would find him, late at night, slumped in an easy chair, drink in hand, listening to Judy Garland on the radio with tears in his eyes. His daughter Diana recalls there was more sadness than usual at the house during that time. "Mom didn't want me staying with friends because she wanted me at home because she was lonely," she recalls. "If there were any problems, I expected Crawford and Cynthia to take care of them. Of everything, I found my mother crying a lot during that time."[117]

Gordon's hobby more and more had become alcohol — alcohol as his stress mechanism, his release to sentimentality. Alcohol had always been part of his life, but now it appeared to be taking over his life. The workaholic was becoming an alcoholic.

> *The pressures on him were inestimable, adds his son Craw-*
> *ford. He simply didn't have the emotional maturity to man-*
> *age all the responsibility. He was a man that had to be in*
> *control. Of all things at all times. He was always trying to*
> *control everything my sisters and I did, our schools, where we*
> *went on holiday. It got to be that we were afraid to tell him*
> *anything for fear of him trying to take control of the situation*
> *and manage it in the way he saw fit.*
>
> *I remember one time he came home with Fred Smye. He had*
> *been in New York and he'd bought my sister Cynthia a dress.*
> *She was about 15 years old at the time and he wanted her to*
> *put the dress on right away and show Mr. Smye. My sister*
> *adamantly refused the request and my father was furious. Just*
> *because she wasn't ready to put a silly dress on when he was.*[118]

The pressure was getting to Crawford Gordon and people were noticing. His devoted wife Mary noticed most of all. Dinner parties were almost obligatory for a man in Gordon's position but he quite literally hated them. There were many of them in the summer of 1958 and most of Mary's time was taken up apologizing to the many people her husband had offended during the evening.

Officials at the plant noticed things as well. His periodic absences had forced board chairman Wilf Curtis to manage meetings more often; Gordon's secretary, Gloria Collinson, became an authority on making excuses for him and even Fred Smye discussed his concerns for his friend with a number of people.

In late July, Gordon booked a cruise on the *Queen Elizabeth* to visit Sir Roy Dobson in England. Getting away might do him good, he thought, and a trip to England was just the tonic. When he did return to Canada a few weeks later, he did feel better, although his arguments with Mary continued even more frequently in the family home at 44 Park Lane Circle. Now, however, they weren't the usual ones about working too much, staying away from home too much, drinking too much. These new arguments had to do with Gordon's recent trip to England and the young lady he had met on the *Queen Elizabeth*. He had been completely smitten from the very first "hello." English by birth, worldly by nature, wise and alluring in her sophistication, her name was Gabrielle Littlehales Raphael, but to her friends she went by the café society nickname of "Billie."

Within a week of his return, Gordon moved out of the Park Lane Circle home and into the company estate at Briarcrest and soon began divorce proceedings. "In the end," recalls his son Crawford, "he just walked out of the house and that was it. It was *his* wish to divorce, not hers."[119] Mary was given $60,000 and appropriate alimony, which ended up being the bare minimum, and by 1964, was in arrears. With the money Mary Gordon purchased a house for $46,000 at 61 Chestnut Park Road. With two daughters, Cynthia 19, and Diana 16, still at home, for the first time in her life Mary Gordon would have to find herself a job.

"She really needed to do something to get on with her life," recalls her son Crawford. "She certainly didn't have the security of cash flow from my father by any means. Bert Willoughby, a real estate agent and friend of my father's approached her with the belief women would be very good at selling real estate so he offered her a job."[120] Mary took the job and went on to become one of the most successful real estate agents in Toronto.

For the rest of her life she called herself Mary Tierney Gordon. She would never remarry.

Gordon had purchased the house on Park Lane Circle for $169,000 in 1954 from the widow of Major James Hahn, who had been his boss at English Electric and John Inglis. Soon after he separated from Mary, Sir Roy Dobson offered to increase his salary from $100,000 to $150,000. Gordon refused but agreed to take a salary of $125,000 if A. V. Roe would buy his Park Lane Circle house for the same price ($169,000) he had paid the Hahn family six years before.

For a while, at least, his temporary home would be Briarcrest.

DIEF AND THE DEATH OF THE ARROW

While Gordon was in England, the debate over the Arrow and Iroquois raged in the press, in the armed forces and in Parliament. The new Conservative government of John Diefenbaker was painfully aware that they had inherited a very costly program from the Liberals that seemed to being going nowhere, except to get even more costly. The thirst for information by the Diefenbaker Cabinet on what was going on at Malton was matched only by the thirst for information by A. V. Roe Canada executives on what was going on in Ottawa.

> *The three Conservative members in the area all had our little organization feeding us information, recalls former Conservative MP John Pallet. We didn't deal with company officials: the people I was interested in were the shop stewards and the guys on the floor … All the fellows on the airframe would tell me about the engines; the fellows on the engines would tell me about the airframe … It wasn't what I wanted to hear, however; I wanted to hear this was a superb aircraft and I found it wasn't a superb aircraft and this was very disturbing to me.*
>
> *What was wrong? They developed a new engine and a new airframe, the only time ever that's been tried. It's like wearing two left shoes; it looks distinctive, but it isn't too bright.*[121]

By end of the summer of 1958 Crawford Gordon decided to take on the government over the Arrow issue. Buoyed by his new relationship with Billie, his new-found freedom from Mary, and irritated about hearing of Fred Smye's meeting with Conservative Cabinet ministers and Pearkes' comment "why don't you build automobiles or something?" Gordon decided to go and see the prime minister himself — face to face. "Someone's got to take on the son of a bitch in Ottawa," he barked to Fred Smye, "and I'm just the one to do it."[122]

From the new company corporate head office on University Avenue in Toronto, Gordon's secretary was able to get an appointment for her boss to meet with Diefenbaker on the afternoon of September 17, 1958. Fred Smye drafted a brief entitled, "The Arrow Program" in which he attempted to outline in simple terms for the prime minister just what effect the Arrow program would have on the country as a whole. In the brief Smye "attempted to turn the effects of the expenditures [in the Arrow and Iroquois programs] back to the government through direct and indirect taxation" and also outlined possible "alternative projects" the company might undertake in the event of cancellation.

Should the program be cancelled, wrote Smye in dramatic fashion, the move would "destroy one of the free world's most progressive and advanced technological organizations," and, "virtually eliminate any future opportunity for Canada to regain a position of leadership in this field." As well, it would create "catastrophic unemployment," and "deprive this country of an effective Canadian-created component of its national defence which cannot be more adequately replaced from non-Canadian sources."[123] Smye then had the briefs bound in brown leather and had copies made for the prime minister and Cabinet.

With Smye working on the brief, Pat Kelly worked on Gordon for what might well have been the most important meeting of his life. First, said Kelly, we'll fly to Ottawa instead of taking the train in order to arrive fresh. Second, no drinking before the meeting, and no smoking in front of the non-smoking prime minister. Third, try and act orderly. Remember he wasn't meeting with C.D. Howe, he was meeting with the Prime Minister of Canada.

Kelly might as well have been talking to a wall. Gordon refused every one of his recommendations. He boarded the train for Ottawa and immediately ordered himself a drink from the club car and lit a cigar. Five hours later Gordon arrived at the prime minister's office, "bombed" and "in no shape for solid conversation."[124]

To add to the situation, Kelly had to scurry back to the train station in an attempt to retrieve Smye's leather-bound briefs which Gordon had forgotten on the train. And if those complications weren't bad enough, Diefenbaker was tied up, leaving Gordon waiting impatiently in the hallway for almost two hours, his indignation growing with every tick of the clock.

When Diefenbaker was finally free, Gordon charged in to meet the prime minister of Canada. In an adjoining office, Conservative MP John Pallet witnessed a meeting he would remember years later. "Gordon was rude, incoherent, like a person demented," recalls Pallet.[125]

Refusing to sit or let Diefenbaker say a word Gordon launched into his tirade. The prime minister was shocked. Here he was the most powerful political figure in the country, being lectured to by one of the most powerful industrialists in the country. Waving his cigar, and reeking of Scotch, Gordon pounded on the prime minister's desk demanding a guarantee that the Arrow program would go ahead. When Gordon continued to shout and pound, Diefenbaker threatened to have him forcibly removed from the office if he didn't settle down. "He [Gordon] was acting very childish over a problem that was quite serious," recalls John Pallett, "like a kid who was having his toy taken away from him."[126]

Years later the prime minister would recall the confrontation this way: "Crawford Gordon was a noisy fellow who thought when I saw his physical dimensions that fear should overwhelm me. It was really nothing ... He swept in and was blatantly noisy and he swept out." Diefenbaker also recalled that Gordon repeatedly pounded on his desk in a blustery fashion until he was warned he might hurt himself.[127]

At that point, Gordon turned and stomped out, cigar ash flying and coat-tails flaring behind him. In the hall Gordon muttered to a colleague, "We'll turn it around,"[128] but when he called Smye later he described the meeting as the most devastating experience of his life."[129] That 20-minute meeting had sealed the fate of the Arrow.

"C.D. Howe was where Crawford got his strength," recalled Ron Adey years later. "But to be able to go to Diefenbaker and tell Dief what he thought, — well Diefenbaker was just as big and just as heavy."[130]

"I have often wondered if it was really necessary for my father to have created an ambience of 'Fuck You' right off the bat with Diefenbaker," reflects Gordon's stepson Stephen. "Dief was nothing if not spiteful and Crawford was nothing if not angry."[131]

And then six days later, on September 23, the prime minister spoke in the House of Commons and made a number of announcements on the defence policy of Canada, three of which had to do with the Arrow program. The Astra and Sparrow missile-fire control programs, destined to be the Arrow's armament system, were to be terminated; the decision to order the Arrow into production would be postponed but development work on the aircraft would be allowed to continue; and, the entire Arrow program would come under a complete review and a decision made on the program would be put off until March 1959. "To cut off the Arrow program now," said Diefenbaker, "would immobilize the industry."[132]

Although taken aback by the announcement, Gordon presented an air of calmness. "Our situation remains unchanged..." he told *The Globe and Mail*. "I feel confident the Arrow will be ordered into production March 31 when the government reviews its defence expenditures. Although we are in a state of gloom over the government's announcement, nothing could be further from the truth that the Avro and Orenda will close down, throwing thousands out of work."[133]

In private, however, away from the public spotlight, A. V. Roe executives in general, and Crawford Gordon in particular, were quietly panicking. For seven years now the company had been on a roll and the September 23 announcement was nothing short of a crisis. In the executive suites at Malton, entire worlds were turned upside down. Information was sparse, office politics was aggravated and journalists beseiged the company with dozens of phone calls every day.

In these kinds of situations, says John Burke, a corporate crisis specialist, "a tremendous bunker mentality develops. And corporate images, with lives longer than any crisis, can become perilously fragile. You're suddenly living in a fishbowl. You have to understand the controlled environment a chief executive normally works in. He's in control. He has immediate access to information. He has time to reflect. Executives are accustomed to giving orders, not patiently answering questions. They're accustomed to sitting with small groups where people say 'yes' pretty readily. Come a crisis, normally obscure executives are cast into the political limelight like so many politicians."[134]

When an organization like A. V. Roe Canada was faced with losing its two key programs in the fall of 1958, it exaggerated the political aspects of the way in which it operated. The immediate response was denial; companies don't want to believe the worst, and A. V. Roe was no different. It embarked on one of the largest public relations campaigns in Canadian industrial history in an effort to save the Arrow. Even Gordon was convinced the Cabinet would reprieve the program, much like a governor reprieves a prisoner who is about to go to the electric chair, at the last moment, in Hollywood movies.

In the months leading up to Christmas, A. V. Roe executives, led by Gordon, did just about everything they could to get into the press and extol the virtues of the Arrow and how vital it was to Canadian defence. No stone was unturned. The company talked about themselves at every opportunity: how the company was worth over $600,000 a year in salaries and taxes to Toronto Township; how 1958 was the company's greatest growth period yet with earnings up 15 per cent; how the company pumped over $300 million into the Canadian economy every year; why the company felt obligated to donate over $100,000 to the victims of the Springhill, Nova Scotia mining disaster; how company exports totaled $52 million through its Orenda engines being used in West Germany, South Africa and Columbia; how Canadian-built CF-100s were flying with the Belgian Air Force; how the last CF-100 number 692 had rolled off the assembly line.

Living alone at Briarcrest, Gordon's interest in the company seemed to be dwindling more and more at a time when it should have been quite the opposite. There were many trips to New York to see Billie, and the occasional visit to see Audrey, although these lacked the intensity of earlier years. Billie was the woman in his life now, and it was with her that his future would lie.

Christmas and New Year's were not quite as festive as they would normally be for A. V. Roe Canada that holiday season of 1958-59, and with good reason. The third largest company in Canada, with a long and continuous relationship with the government of Canada, had no idea what was going on. The government-threatened review of the program was rapidly approaching, no one knew if the plane was to be ordered into production or not and the company's CEO was more interested in spending time in New York than in Malton.

On the day before New Year's Eve, and with Gordon away, Fred Smye composed what would turn out to be a final pre-cancellation letter to Raymond O'Hurley at Defence Production regarding some bottom-line costs on the Arrow program. The company was prepared to guarantee a fly-away price per Arrow of $3.75 million without fire control and missiles for 37 aircraft, not including the money invested in the development of the aircraft; with fire control and missiles the price per Arrow would be $4.3 million not including development costs. It was a desperate last move for a company in guaranteeing the price of an aircraft in an atmosphere of unknowns.

In Ottawa Lester Pearson, the Opposition leader, asked C.D. Howe, now retired, for advice on how the Liberal Party should position itself with the program that was beginning to catch the imagination of the entire country. Howe's reply surprised Pearson. "There is no doubt in my mind that the CF-105 should be terminated," wrote the former Minister of Everything. "Costs are completely out of hand ... I had then [in 1957] recommended that the project be terminated due to runaway costs ... results of test flights have been far from conclusive.... Subsequent expenditures on both aircraft and engine were definitely an unemployment relief measure, and an expensive one."[135]

In the East Block, Cabinet had been advised the previous fall that the cost of completing the 37 aircraft in the development contract would amount to approximately $340 million, and this would not include fire control and missiles. After March 31 an additional $260 would probably be required, bringing the total in at about $600 million. Aviation writer Jim Hornick's comparison with the building of the St. Lawrence Seaway was starting to ring true.

But costs were only part of the problem. Many members of Cabinet truly believed that missiles were the only way to go and that the Arrow was indeed obsolete. And even today, the obsolete argument is one of the most curious aspects of the Arrow debate.

The main argument against the Arrow, recalls former Transportation Minister George Hees, was that by the time we took over the government in 1957, the Avro Arrow had become obsolete. Now this plane was designed around 1952 for the previous Liberal government, but by 1957 and '58 it had become completely outdated for this reason: it was designed to fly up and intercept Russian bombers flying at a maximum altitude of 25,000 feet. And so the plane was designed with a fuel capacity, and a missile capacity to fire into the Russian planes, that would get it up to 25,000 feet and allow the plane to return safely to its starting point. The trouble was that by '57/'58, when we took over, the Russians had developed a bomber that would fly at not 25,000 feet, but 50,000 feet. And so, of course, our interceptor, the Arrow, would have to fly to 50,000 feet into the air, discharge its missiles into the Russian bomber, destroy the atomic bombs coming across at the time, and be able to return to earth.

But with the design that had been put into the plane, it would not have been possible for the plane to fly up and back. It would be able to fly up to 50,000 feet, then it would have expended all of its fuel, and the plane would of course, crash when it returned to earth to land. And that was of course not a practical idea at all ... The Arrow wouldn't do the job ... Now the plane was obsolete and there's no question about it, it was obsolete, it couldn't do the job. Not one of those planes could ever have taken off to do the job they were supposed to do because you can't send a plane up to intercept a bomber, and then know that the plane and the pilot are going to crash on return to earth.[136]

As absurd as this statement was at the time, this reflection by one of the most senior conservative Cabinet ministers becomes even more incredible with the passing of time. It angers and astonishes many people still.

Cabinet had already decided the fate of the Arrow program. In fact, a decision had been made the previous November. The cancellation was postponed until the spring to allow the workers to keep working through the winter months. It seems that C.D. Howe had been right after all about the Arrow program being "an unemployment relief measure."

By February 20, 1959, some despair and lots of anxiety had replaced the air of confidence that had once been the very fabric of A. V. Roe. Everyone knew what the headlines were saying, that there was a debate going on about their plane, but the vast majority of the employees never thought the program would be cancelled, trimmed down maybe, but never cancelled. After all, the president of A. V. Roe Canada was still Crawford Gordon. He had worked wonders before, had never failed, and he would work wonders again. Nothing was further from the truth on that cold February day.

At 9:30 in the morning, John Diefenbaker rose in the House of Commons to speak at length about one facet of the national defence of Canada — the Avro Arrow. He talked about the Arrow as an aircraft that had shown promise but had been "overtaken by events."[137] He questioned some aspects of the Arrow's performance as not being quite up to what was needed and he reviewed the costs of the program which didn't quite jive with the figures Fred Smye had put forth in his proposal to O'Hurley in late December. "The conclusion arrived at," said the prime minister of Canada, "is that the development of the aircraft and the Iroquois engine should be terminated now."[138] Cabinet had decided not to wait until March 31.

At the same time Diefenbaker was on his feet in the House, Gordon Hunter from DDP called Fred Smye to inform him of the decision and Smye immediately headed for Briarcrest to tell Gordon. Gordon was still asleep, having spent much of the night before trying to contact Tory Cabinet ministers Michael Starr (Labour) and Donald Fleming (Finance) but without success. He had left orders with the housekeeping staff not to be awakened except for an emergency. At 10:45 a.m. that emergency arrived with Fred Smye.

Smye and Gordon began calling company executives to convene at Briarcrest to try and figure out what to do. At the plants, the word was spreading through the assembly bays and offices like wildfire, phone lines jammed up, and people were walking everywhere, like ants across an anthill looking for any bit of information.

At 11:42 a.m. two telexes arrived at exactly the same time at Orenda Engines and Avro Aircraft with exactly the same message: "Take notice that your contracts ... are hereby terminated ... you shall cease all work immediately, terminate subcontracts ... place no further subcontracts or orders and instruct all your subcontractors and suppliers to take similar action...."

At Briarcrest Fred Smye asked that the telex be read over the phone to him. Many of the company executives had already arrived and some, according to Pat Kelly, were already "quite loaded."[139]

"We kicked around for a while what to do," recalls Fred Smye. "I was the one who pressed the idea of giving notice to the whole works, not Gordon. I mean the telex was clear: no further contracts, incur no further costs. To me the message was very clear: we'd have to lay everyone off."[140]

Gordon then suggested that everyone reconvene in the boardroom at Malton. It was a scene they'd never forget. People were walking around in a daze, many were crying, the sounds of production had stopped: no rivet guns, no saws, no typewriters, no hammers, just the milling around of people and a production line at a halt.

Finally at a little after 4:00 p.m., Gordon sat down in front of the company Public Address system and declared:

> *Following the prime minister's statement, we have received news from the government instructing us to immediately cease all work on the Arrow and Iroquois programs at Malton and by all suppliers and subcontractors. As a result, notice of termination of employment is being given to all employees of Avro Aircraft and Orenda Engines pending a full assessment of the impact of the prime minister's statement on our operation.*

We profoundly regret this action but have no alternative since the company received no prior notice of the decision, and therefore we were unable to plan any orderly adjustments.[141]

By now the afternoon papers had hit the streets. "SCRAP ARROW," said *The Toronto Star*, "No other work for makers of arrow or engines. *The Toronto Telegram* echoed "EVERYBODY OUT UNTIL AVRO'S POSITION CLEAR."

By the end of the day 14,528 Avro and Orenda employees had been sent home. A few would be called back to work on CF-100 overhaul projects and other maintenance-type work, but the vast majority would never see the plant again. At shift change at 5:30 p.m. some employees still milled about the plant gates, some because of habit, some because of shock. Most of the company executives had gone home to think about their future as well. Crawford Gordon returned to Briarcrest for one more appointment with his bottle of Scotch.

THE AFTERMATH

By the following Monday, February 23, the shock of what had happened on the previous Friday was beginning to settle in. It wasn't often in the Canada of 1959 that the disappearance of a weekly payroll totaling $1,162,240 — equalling the purchasing power of an Oshawa, a Brantford or a Kitchener — goes unnoticed.

"It would have been better," commented Reeve Chris Tonks from the borough of York, "to keep these men on the production line instead of dumping them on the relief line."[142] From Reeve Oscar Waffle of Etobicoke: "It almost looks as if somebody is trying to destroy our aircraft industry and our national defence."[143] Reeve Jack Allen was more succinct: "It [cancelling the Arrow] was a stupid decision."[144]

However, the reaction to the lay-offs was not all negative. A. V. Roe stock only dropped half a point from 12 1/4 to 11 3/4. And a *Globe and Mail* poll just days after the cancellation indicated that one out of three Canadians were "unconcerned" about the decision.[145] Even

Executive Decision magazine took aim at A.V. Roe executives, saying they "knew very well the Arrow would be cancelled and yet sat around for months and did nothing...."

On Monday, February 23, Gordon and a couple of the A. V. Roe executives got their chance to speak to the media at the corporate offices on University Avenue. "Gordon, looking flushed and strained, opened the conference by announcing that only 12 men were called back to work that day, saying that the vice-president of manufacturing may be asked to become a foreman tomorrow. He offered his sympathies to the men and women thrown out of work and reiterated the fact that the company had not been forewarned of the cancellation."[146]

He then concluded his remarks by saying the company had meetings planned with the government to talk about some alternative proposals to keep the men working and the company in operation. The proposals included everything from the design of a jet transport for the RCAF, to the continued development of the company's flying saucer project for the USAF (known as the Avrocar), to working on a nuclear power project, to space exploration. A mere grasping at straws.

"What about the lay-offs ?" asked a reporter. "Did you really have to do it?"
"We had no alternative," snapped a red-faced Fred Smye. "We didn't bloody well do it for fun!"[147]

The next day, the prime minister finally made a statement admitting that although the Arrow was "outstanding," it had been "overtaken by events" and "would have been obsolete by the time it was ready for squadron use. No one advocates building buggies in the age of motor cars." Later he would say that there is no purpose in manufacturing horse collars when horses no longer exist.[148]

Years later Diefenbaker would be more reflective, saying that, "Some people talk about courage. Well, we took a stand in reference to the Arrow. No one wanted to take that stand ... As I look back on it, I think it was one of the decisions that was right. Here was an instru-

ment beautiful in appearance, powerful, a tribute to Canadian production ... This instrument that contributed little, in the changing
order of things, to our national defence."[149]

That same day Gordon and Smye met with members of the Diefenbaker Cabinet including ministers Donald Fleming, George Hees,
Michael Starr, Raymond O'Hurley and George Pearkes to discuss the
future of A. V. Roe. The prime minister was absent and Gordon's
contribution to the meeting was minimal at best. Most of the talking
was done by Smye. Several ministers agreed that some of the company's proposals had promise, while others looked rather doubtful.
They agreed to report to the prime minister on the results of the
meeting.

"There are some who believe," said *The Ottawa Gazette*, "that the personality clash between Dief and Gordon may have had something to
do with the decision. It made it impossible for the government and
the company to cooperate fully."[150] The personality clash continued
with the prime minister and Gordon snapping and bickering at every
opportunity. But it wasn't really a personality clash at all, but more
like a sparring between two unlikely adversaries, both mercurial, separated only by geography, constituency and stubborn pride.

"The company," argued Gordon, "has repeatedly proposed ... alter-
nate programs. However the government has not seen fit to discuss
these matters or consult with us in any way."[151]

Diefenbaker responded by charging the A. V. Roe management with
"the unwarranted and unjustifiable dismissal of its entire working
force. It was done for the purpose of embarrassing the government."[152] He claimed that the company's management knew the
Arrow was doomed. "I will not say that they knew the exact date, but
they knew what the decision was and that it was unchangeable."[153]
Despite all the media attention and speculation around the fate of the
Arrow, A.V. Roe executives never really felt the Arrow would be cancelled entirely. They truly felt the plane would be ordered into production although perhaps not in sufficient numbers to equip all
RCAF squadrons. That was all they would need to buy time in order
to secure other contracts for both aviation and non-aviation products.

"Our company was told that the decision of whether or not to proceed with the project would be taken by the end of March," added Sir Roy Dobson, "Suddenly, out of the blue ... in such circumstances what could the company do?"[154]

By this time, however, it didn't matter that much to Crawford Gordon. He knew a lost cause when he saw one. All of his energy now focused on his new relationship with Gabrielle Littlehaus, his Billie. Leaving most of the final battles at A. V. Roe to Fred Smye, Gordon rarely showed up for work after February 20, 1959, even less than before. In the spring he moved out of Briarcrest and took an apartment in Toronto and commuted on an almost weekly basis to New York to see Billie.

"You know I never really thought it was anything more than an affair," recalls former secretary Gloria Collinson. "I used to find these notes they used to write back and forth to each other. I found it rather fascinating because he used to call her 'my little sparrow' and they shared a favourite song, I think it was 'Que Sera Sera.'"[155]

There were still those within the company, however, who felt the Arrow program would be revised and were prepared to exhaust almost every option to see that it happened. Wilf Curtis, chairman of the board, was one; John Tory, the company's legal advisor, was another, and a third was the man who had started it all 14 years before, Sir Roy Dobson. With Gordon now largely absent, Curtis had taken to running the company. Dobson stepped into the fray, and he and John Tory met with the prime minister in Ottawa on March 3 in a clear attempt to heal the breach between the government and the company. During the visit, Dobson was disturbed to hear from a number of people on their dissatisfaction with Gordon, the man that many people believed Dobson looked upon as a son. For them it was difficult to tell the old man, and it was difficult for him to hear what they had to say. The September 1958 confrontation with Diefenbaker didn't help Gordon's cause and Dobson actually came away from the meeting with a plan that he truly thought might save the Arrow program: offer up the head of Crawford Gordon.

GORDON'S RESIGNATION

By the end of March, 2,500 Avro and Orenda workers had been called back to work, 500 had found other jobs, 750 had gone to the United States, 410 had returned to England and 10,000 were still looking. Some employees had even started their own companies. This was also the end of the federal government's fiscal year and, for the first time, the figures on government investment in the Arrow and Iroquois programs were released. To date over $132 million had been invested in the Iroquois program and over $247 million in the Arrow program for a total of $379 million for an aircraft that never went into production and for an engine that was never married to the airplane.

"As a fighting instrument of war," David Golden, the former deputy minister of Defence Production would tell the CBC years later, "which must include an aircraft, an engine, and a sophisticated fire control system, then, of course, there never was an Arrow...."[156]

By the end of April all the Arrow prototypes had been sold to a scrap dealer and were being cut up including the jigs, tools and the dies to build her. Since the cancellation in February, one executive after another had resigned, leaving little of the management team that had once run the flagship of Canadian aviation. Now, with the Arrow gone, the assembly bays empty and the place almost deserted, the flagship was listing so severely, few saw little hope of saving her. Few, that is, except Sir Roy Dobson who would "have done just about anything to save the Arrow program"[157] — even if it meant disowning the man he treated like a son.

On June 17 he did just that when he wrote to the prime minister that he had asked for Crawford Gordon's resignation. "I have been very dissatisfied with his work and his actions," he wrote, "which have not been in the best interests of the company and the country."[158] He went on to say Gordon's resignation would be effective on July 2 and that he himself would assume Gordon's duties until a successor had been chosen. "Dobson had had it with Crawford at this point," recalls Gordon's former secretary, Gloria Collinson. "He felt tremendously betrayed in the end over Crawford and Mary separating, the fact that Crawford was drinking too much and the earlier playing around with Howard Hughes."[159]

When he met the press soon afterwards, Dobson said Gordon's resignation was due to an "irreconcilable difference of opinion over matters of policy. Words cannot adequately express the regret I feel at this turn of events. Crawford Gordon has always been one of my best personal friends and, I believe one of the most competent young industrialists Canada has produced. He has made a valuable contribution to the growth of the company and, indeed to the development of Canada."[160]

"My association with A. V. Roe Canada has been most satisfying," responded Gordon on his resignation, "in that I believe the company has contributed and will continue to contribute something of real and lasting value to Canada's industrial progress. The credit for this must go to the many thousands of men and women with whom I have worked in the last eight years. I thank them sincerely for the help, cooperation and friendship they have given me, for, in the final analysis, it is they who are responsible for what has been accomplished."

* * * *

Theodore Roosevelt once wrote that it was not the critic that counted, not the man who points out how the strong man stumbled or where the doer of deeds could have done them better. The credit belongs to the man who is actually in the arena, whose face is marred by dust and sweat and blood; who strives valiantly; who errs and comes up short again; who knows the great enthusiasm, the great devotions, and spends himself in a worthy cause; who at best knows in the end the triumphs of high achievement, and who at the worst, if he fails, at least fails while daring greatly, so that his place shall never be with those cold and timid souls who know neither defeat nor victory.

Crawford Gordon's last day at A. V. Roe Canada was Friday June 30, 1959. By then most of the management team had gone. Gordon's pals Walter McLachlan and Bill Dickie had left in April. Jim Floyd had left two weeks earlier, returning to England. Fred Smye would hang on for another month and be fired on July 31. And once again Gordon was prepared to walk away from yet another challenge without so much as a whimper. Like CGE, Munitions and Supply and Inglis, A. V. Roe was simply one more place to walk away from and not look back.

It didn't take him long that Friday to clean out his office at the corporate headquarters on University Avenue and by noon he was ready to leave. As in the past, no one was there to see him off — not Dobson, no remaining management committee members, no board members, no one. Looking around for someone to have a farewell drink with, he spotted one of the executive secretaries, training another young secretary who had just joined the company.

"Come out for a farewell drink with me, will you?" he asked. "And bring your friend with you." The three walked over to a company hang-out, the Lord Simcoe Hotel, and Gordon ordered a round of drinks, and over that one drink, for the next couple of hours, he reminisced with the two women about his years at A. V. Roe, the challenges, the people and all.

At about 3:00 he put the women in a cab, said goodbye and walked down King Street.

"We were in tears," she recalls. "And the girl I was with says 'Oh, he's so lonely' as we watched him walk away. And that was the last time I saw him. He never came back, even for a visit, to A. V. Roe."[161]

The bull had left his china shop.

SPRAWLING $300,000,000
A. V. ROE EMPIRE

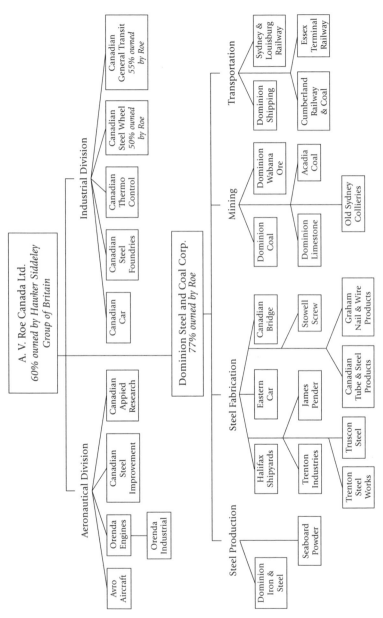

A. V. Roe Canada Ltd at the height of its industrial might in 1958. From a one product company to 31 corporations in 7 years almost single handedly assembled by Crawford Gordon. In Canada the company lived its motto during the 1950's — "The next big step."

Chapter Six

THE FINAL YEARS (1959-67)

BILLIE

*G*abrielle Kathleen Littlehales, Gabrielle de la Volta, Gabrielle Raphael, Billie de la Volta, Billie — all one and the same — and, in the summer of 1959, she became Mrs. Crawford Gordon.

Café society, today as then, is exemplified by superficial living, clusters of Martini-soaked individuals insensitive to human values, subscribing to the code that if you're rich, amusing and witty, we'll love you. "You're a great sport, old boy," but turn old, boring or poor, then we won't have time for you — you're out of the loop. Cocktails after tennis, dinners at the club, rubbing shoulders with the famous and nearly famous, and if you are in the movies, all the better. Taking most of their best dialogue from a Cole Porter melody or a Noel Coward play and characterized in such films as *High Society* or the *Thin Man* series, the world becomes their games room where bets are made and partners exchanged as casually as changing one's clothes.

Born Gabrielle Kathleen Littlehales in England on Christmas Day 1912, Billie was two years less a day older than Crawford. She was the daughter of the Countess de la Volta, an English woman who had married an Italian count but had about as much of the disposition of a countess as a sheeny man collecting bones and rags on the streets of London. Billie had been schooled in Paris, gambled in Monte Carlo and was a full participant in the café society of the 1930s and 40s. "She didn't have the money other members of café society had," recalls her son Stephen. "But she was pretty."[1]

At the age of 19, on a dare, she bet her girlfriends she could get a part in a new Cicely Courtneidge film, *Everybody Dance* which was being filmed at the Gainsborough Studios near her home. She rented a Rolls Royce, drove to the studio, walked into the casting director's office and demanded a part in the film. When he asked which films she had been in, she listed a number of French films in her best Parisian accent. The casting director, not wanting to reveal his ignorance, gave her a part. When Director Charles Reisner, an American, asked her where she was born, she answered Birmingham.

"In Alabama?" he asked.
"No," she answered hotly. "I mean the REAL Birmingham!"

One of the scenes in the film called for Billie to cry but she couldn't do it, prompting Reisner to demand: "Think of the saddest thing you can or I'll fire you!" Ten minutes later real tears came.

"What did you think of?" asked Reisner.
"Haile Selassie," was the reply.[2]

Billie's first husband was stockbroker Stephen Frederick Raphael, educated at Eton, gainfully employed in his family's financial firm, R. Raphael & Sons, founded in 1787. Between 1935 and 1955 Stephen Raphael could claim to be the "world's greatest backgammon player" and with money in his pocket and beautiful new wife Billie on his arm, they moved to Hollywood in the late 1930s and gave up the café society of Europe for the café society of America's movie capital. Before long Raphael was chumming around with the likes of Errol Flynn when he and his wife weren't flitting off to New York, Paris, Venice and Monte Carlo. "I never saw my father play a competitive sport," recalls son Stephen. "I remember walking with him once over 36 holes of golf. He wasn't golfing but was taking bets on every hole and the outcome of the game. He was a gambler and a playboy in every sense."[3]

It didn't take Billie long to realize that gambling in Las Vegas was different from gambling in Monte Carlo. On her first trip to the roulette table in Vegas, one of the bouncers approached her.

"Hey lady," he said. "The dames are down at the other end."
"Oh, thank you so very much indeed," she replied. "Would you mind telling me where the *men* are standing then?"
"Hey, you're OK lady!" answered the bouncer.

In 1940 Billie and Stephen gave birth to their only child Stephen. Soon afterward Stephen Sr. enlisted in the British Army out of a sense of duty and for the next five years the only action he saw was in the bedroom. Billie and her son moved to Nassau in the Bahamas and although the younger Stephen had never met his father, he was constantly asking his mother about him to which she would reply, "He's off fighting Hitler." When the elder Stephen returned from the war, his son was full of questions.

"Daddy," he asked, "tell me about the war, how you beat Hitler," and the elder Stephen replied: "It was awful, I really don't want to talk about it all."

"But Daddy," pressed the young Stephen, "what was the worst thing that happened to you?"

"The worst thing," came the reply, "was being sent to basic training in a place called Edmonton, Alberta!"

"What was the best thing Daddy?" continued young Stephen.

"The best thing was being stationed in Cairo and connecting with one of King Farouk's mistresses who had the only source of hot and cold running water to be found anywhere."[4]

Stephen and Billie's incompatibility eventually came to a head, and they divorced in 1947. Billie achieved landed immigrant status in the United States and took an apartment in a fashionable section of New York, near Park Avenue. The alimony Billie received allowed her to place young Stephen in boarding schools and continue with the café society lifestyle she knew so well. This meant travelling to Europe at least once a year, always in first-class quarters on either the *Queen Mary* or *Queen Elizabeth*. Since Stephen's father had no interest in his son, or any children for that matter, young Stephen always accompanied his mother on the trips when he wasn't escaping into his only passion — watching Hollywood movies, particularly musicals.

He did cross the Atlantic once with his father on the *Queen Elizabeth*. On that trip young Stephen met Jimmy Hanson, who later became Lord Hanson. With him at the dinner table was his girlfriend, Audrey Hepburn, just beginning to make a name for herself in Hollywood. The next year, 1958, young Stephen ran into Jimmy Hanson again on the *Queen Elizabeth*, but this time he was dining with someone Stephen didn't recognize. Hanson called the young man over to the table. "Stephen Raphael, I'd like you to meet Crawford Gordon."

"Now for Crawford to be seen with the likes of Hanson," Stephen would recall years later, "and spending at least a week travelling on the *Queen Elizabeth* at the height of the Arrow program [1958] indicated to me he wasn't quite the workaholic he once was."[5] The next time young Stephen would see Crawford Gordon, Gordon would be romancing his mother, Billie.

> *It was just before we left New York on the Queen Elizabeth, recalls Billie Gordon. I went into the smoking lounge and he was there and he immediately asked the chief steward if he could buy me a drink. The chief steward was a friend of mine and somewhat protective of a single woman travelling alone and said, 'No she won't accept a drink from anyone.'*
>
> *Later on when I was in my room dressing for dinner. The purser called and said to come down for dinner because he wanted me to meet someone. And that someone turned out to be Crawford Gordon.*[6]

Soon after Crawford Gordon returned from meeting Billie on that Atlantic crossing the summer of 1958, he left his wife and family and moved into the A. V. Roe company estate, Briarcrest. During the height of the Arrow debates, when his attention should have been on what was happening in Malton, Gordon was carrying on a long-distance romance. That began taking up more and more of his time and attention. He visited New York frequently during the fall of 1958 and the summer of 1959. The day after he was fired from A. V. Roe by Sir Roy Dobson, Gordon closed up his Toronto apartment, took the few belongings he had and flew to New York. Within 48 hours, Billie and Crawford were married and on the *Queen Elizabeth*, bound for Europe. They would be gone for months. When word of the marriage reached Toronto, few were surprised. Those who really knew Gordon realized that he was a loner who hated to be alone. "Billie might have got his last years," one of Gordon's friends reflected, "but Mary got his best years."[7]

But some people saw Gordon's marriage and his leaving Canada as nothing short of a tactical retreat. "He was humiliated," recalls his son Crawford. "He'd just been fired by Sir Roy Dobson and his pride had taken a terrible beating. You've got nobody to turn to. No job. No friends. When you burn all your bridges and run out of all your options, what do you do? You know there's more to life than Toronto, so you leave the country."[8]

In the spring of 1960 Crawford, Stephen and Billie returned from Europe and moved to Montreal. For the first few weeks the family lived in the fashionable Ritz-Carleton Hotel on Sherbrooke Street and Gordon got his new son a job in the Montreal operation of Dosco, the company he had once bought as part of A. V. Roe Canada.

"I had taken a number of courses in industrial engineering and accounting," recalls Stephen, "but by far most of my business education came from the 'mouth of the boy genius.' He taught me. He got me over the hump of thinking about 'net income' as a concept of real importance and into cash flow and balance sheet analysis. Crawford had a great flair for this."[9]

But by 1960 Crawford Gordon seemed to have lost his great flair for doing business. Gordon's assets upon returning to Montreal amounted to something close to $3 million ($18 million in today's dollars). Some of this was stock he owned, but most of it was cash. He had no income, no business ventures at the time and was paying alimony to his former wife, Mary Gordon in Toronto. Investing in, or buying a company, would seem a logical first move for a man so familiar with such things, but the first thing Gordon did was to buy a house. And quite a house it was. Located at 789 Lexington Avenue in Montreal's fashionable Westmount, it was reputed to be one of the three most opulent and expensive houses in the city at the time. And it was huge — over 6,400 square feet! Gordon paid over half a million dollars ($3 million today) for the house. The taxes alone were $4,200 per year. "The house really wasn't all *that* large," recalls Billie Gordon. "The rooms were very large. It had a billiard room downstairs and a bar, a conservatory and beautiful stairs with marble columns."[10]

"But is this a good way to start your new business career?" wonders stepson Stephen Raphael. "Do you buy a house or do you buy a business? Now I know my mother had a hand in this. My mother knew nothing about money except how to spend it. This is the way she wanted to live, had to live, expected to live."[11]

"Knowing my father," echoes Crawford Gordon III, "this was his way of making a statement. He wanted everyone to know he'd arrived."[12]

BACK TO BUSINESS

With his new family settled in his new house, Gordon started to make it known that he was interested in getting into, or starting up a business. Soon after he bought two companies almost simultaneously; one had to do with travel, the other had to do with trailers.

After leaving A. V. Roe, he would tell the Financial Post, I spent two months touring Europe [on his honeymoon]. I examined a number of companies in the Inner Six [Common Market] and Great Britain. I was convinced that the European market was on the verge of enormous prosperity, much greater than many Europeans seemed to believe.

However I still wanted to live at least half the time in Canada. I set out to plan an operation that would allow me to invest in both areas. I'm sure that Canada can find good markets in Europe, but it has to be very much the old business of a better mousetrap.

My ambition had always been to go into business on my own at 40. Well, I made it at 45. I am not interested in taking on products or companies that I don't really understand.[13]

It took the two businesses he had acquired to prove this to be true.

"He was down in 1960 but he was still acting like an industrialist," says stepson Stephen. "Firing 14,000 [at A.V. Roe] was absolutely horrible for him. He got shot down, not the plane. By 1960 he was starting a self-destruct mode."[14] "It broke him up," adds his wife Billie. "After they cancelled the Arrow he wasn't the same person ... he started drinking heavily...."[15]

Son Crawford put it more bluntly: "He never really worked at coming back. A. V. Roe killed him. I talked with him about this a number of times and he was constantly reflecting on it. He couldn't help it. It was the biggest event of his life. It was the company, not the plane. It had nothing to do with the plane. The plane was just an instrument. His spirit had been shattered."[16]

Crawford Gordon got involved in the travel business with a partner by the name of Leon Parras, who was an insurance salesman with what he thought was an interesting idea. He reasoned that if millions of North Americans could put aside small amounts of money for everything from government bonds to prepaid cemetery plots, then surely they'd be willing to put money aside for a dream vacation. Tourism was on the rise and it was predicted that people would have more leisure time. And what better way to use that leisure time than to go on a vacation.

The concept was simple. It cost three dollars a year to become a member of the scheme. Then members would choose their dream vacation, but because they couldn't afford it all at once, they would deposit so much every month — like a savings account — with the travel agency until the dream vacation was paid for. An added incentive was a monthly draw for a free vacation for two for members.

The idea was that Gordon and Parras would live off the float created by the membership fees generating interest at the bank. Gordon and Parras each invested $12,500 in the scheme, not an excessive amount of money considering Gordon's resources, and the Gordon/Parras Travel Development Corporation was founded. But within 14 months the business had lost $40,000. It seemed that investing in bonds or cemetery plots was quite different than investing in frivolous vacations. Gordon wanted out.

In June 1961 Gordon's stepson Stephen turned 21 and in typical fashion, Gordon threw two birthday parties for him: one in Montreal and the other in the famous Maximes in Paris. When Gordon heard that Stephen had received a $75,000 birthday gift from his father, Stephen Raphael, he immediately offered to sell him the travel business. "Take $25,000 of your money and buy us out," said Gordon. "You can own your very own business."

"Now as an investor I was robbed and cheated," says Stephen. "But as a business experience it was wonderful. I don't think his motive was to get $25,000 from me."[17] As it turned out, it was a good move for Stephen. Within a few months he had turned the business around, even managing to pay himself a salary before selling out in late 1963. He lost some money but ended up doing better at it than his industrialist stepfather.

* * * *

In December 1960 word reached Gordon that C. D. Howe, his mentor, had died in Ottawa. Although the boss and his Boy Wonder hadn't talked all that much in recent years, Gordon was devastated when he heard the news. On January 4, 1961 he attended the funeral at Christ Church Cathedral on Ste. Catherine Street in Montreal, a short distance from his Westmount home. When he returned from the funeral, he draped the ever-present photograph of C.D. on the mantelpiece in black and mourned for a week. The loner was now even more alone.

Crawford was a loner and Billie was happy to be a loner too, recalls her son Stephen. They were happy in their big house. They didn't have a lot of friends and socialized very rarely. There'd be a dinner once a week in the restaurant garden at the Ritz Carleton or a more informal meal at Le Paris restaurant on Ste. Catherine Street West, but mostly they stayed at home.

Billie and Crawford were strangers to Montreal society — fundamentally outsiders. This was not an old Canadian family or Westmount establishment, these people were newcomers.[18]

Old friends from the A.V. Roe days would occasionally visit, although rarely. Fred Smye, Bill Dickie and George Mara would drop in and express sadness at what they saw. They'd say Gordon was living in an unrealistic façade, that he talked about being in business as if he was trying to justify his existence. After all, he had been larger than life, and now he was attempting to make his life better than it was. But his friends sensed a desperation and they came away feeling their old friend was sliding downhill and "had many days of being in bad shape."[19]

* * * *

The Gardner Trailer Company was a small business made up of an office and small manufacturing plant employing some 30 people, operating in two shifts. It made floats for transport trailers — the platforms that allow trucks to carry heavy equipment — and other components for trucks as well. Later they would acquire the distribution rights for Kenworth Trucks in Canada. Gordon bought 100 per cent of the company and hired Larry Hunt to run it for him.

Hunt was a member of the Montreal establishment and, according to some, was the best-dressed man in Montreal. "His suits were tailored in London," recalls Stephen Raphael. "There wasn't anyone in Montreal that could make suits good enough for Larry."[20] Good looking and charming, Hunt knew the trucking trailer industry and everyone in it. In 1961 he was the president of CanCar, an A. V. Roe subsidiary bought by Crawford Gordon some years before, and it was Hunt to whom Crawford would turn to run Gardner Trailers.

> *Problem was, recalls stepson Stephen Raphael, Hunt knew absolutely nothing about industrial engineering. He could not run a factory if you shot his head off. And even he admitted that. He was not a manufacturing guy — he was a deal-maker and salesman.*
>
> *Soon after, Hunt came on board and suddenly expenses started running wildly out of control. And Crawford refused to get involved. He barely made an appearance at the plant and adamantly refused to ride herd on Hunt, even though his company was starting to haemorrhage around him. I remember Hunt lived in this huge estate and on more than one occasion when I visited him, there were Gardner Trailer people cutting the lawn and doing maintenance work around the place. Now whose payroll were they on, Hunt's or Gordon's?*
>
> *Larry might have been a great guy to head the firm — right image, right contacts, he even secured new lines — but you don't ask the best-dressed man in Montreal to control costs.*[21]

Complicating the situation somewhat was the fact that Gordon and Hunt were becoming close friends at a time when Gordon had few friends; Gordon's stepson even dated Hunt's daughter.

Gardner's financial man at the time was Frank Topping, who was the type of guy who probably had no more than three suits, all of which he wore out. He was personally very frugal and being head of finance of a company that was bleeding to death worried him to no end. On many occasions Topping made the trip to Lexington Avenue to tell Gordon quite bluntly that if it continued to run as it was presently his business would self-destruct. Topping even appealed to Gordon's stepson to get the message across.

"[Gordon] was drinking quite heavily at this point," recalls Stephen. "Mostly because he was home all day. Now here's a man who doesn't have an office to go to. And why not? Because he doesn't *want* one. You own 100 per cent of a company and you don't have an office there or even want one?"[22]

But Crawford III explains, almost defends, his father's actions: "He simply didn't have the interest," he adds. "When you've run a company like A. V. Roe, it's like going from a giant to a pipsqueak. You treat it almost with a laissez-faire attitude."[23]

When Stephen Raphael tried to talk to his stepfather about the trailer company, he ran into a brick wall: "But I'd seen something; I knew the company was going down when Topping asked me to talk to Crawford. I had to be very careful. Nobody talked to him about how to run a business; he became very defensive and antagonistic. When I finally told him Gardner was going to kill him financially, his response was: 'What the fuck do you know at 22 years of age about running Gardner Trailers! You don't understand everything, you know!'"[24] But neither did Gordon, it seemed.

THE NOSEDIVE

By early 1963, with his company still losing money, a rapid series of events demonstrated the seriousness of Gordon's business woes. Gordon's personal guarantees, his markers to secure goods and services, were being called or were no longer accepted. His company car, owned by Gardner Trailers, was seized. He had to sell his huge home on Lexington Avenue at a substantial loss and move into a $1200-per-month apartment on Mountain Street near his old Alma Mater, McGill. Soon after, a developer purchased the property, demolished the house, and created six exclusive lots which he sold — one to the Bronfman family. At one point some debt collectors showed up at the apartment and threatened Billie with taking away "their" property, including a television and anything that appeared valuable. Only some quick cheque writing by Gordon on the spot saved the furniture.

By late 1963 Gordon was still the president of Gardner Trailers, which was then losing money more rapidly than ever. Stephen had left home and Billie and Crawford had settled into their new, relatively modest digs on Mountain Street.

The money Gordon brought to Montreal was rapidly drying up because he refused to do anything to stop the haemorrhaging at his trailer company. Most people would have sold out by this time but instead, Gordon did something quite extraordinary. In the spring of 1964 he bought a villa on the French Riveria to announce his membership in the café society.

"If he had sold the house in Westmount and lived modestly in the apartment in Montreal, it would have been good," recalls Stephen. "But he's got a problem. He's facing reality. The business is not going well. Instead of changing courses, he buys a villa on one of the most expensive pieces of real estate on the Mediterranean with two servants and a Rolls Royce."[25]

The home that Gordon purchased on the Mediterranean was the Villa Falcarra near St. Jean Cap Ferrat in the south of France, very close — maybe too close — to the gambling casinos at Monte Carlo. With a business back home losing money hand over fist, instead of doing something about it, Gordon chose to spend his days playing baccarat with Johnny Iannelli, chairman of Fiat, Dino DeLaurentis, the film producer, or Gregory Peck, the actor. When not staying at the villa, the Gordons rented it out to, among others, Sean Connery.

By this time everyone knew Gordon liked to gamble. Years before it had been on golf matches with Fred Smye or football games with his best friend Len Lumbers. He once lost $2,000 on a Toronto Argonaut game and would drop a few bucks here and there on poker and bridge. But now he was really gambling — Monte Carlo gambling — which was steps up from the small amounts lost sitting in the seats watching the Argos play at Varsity Stadium in Toronto. Gordon gambled away his dwindling assets at $5,000 a hand when not cocktailing away the evenings in formal wear. He once boasted to his son Crawford that he had won $42,000 at the bacarat table in one day. What he failed to mention was that he had lost $44,000 the day before.

Gordon would call his financial adviser at Burns-Fry at all hours of the day and night with inconsistent demands that he buy into all sorts of unusual things. The adviser, concerned that some of these requests were quite off the wall, consulted Gordon's best friend Len Lumbers on what to do. Lumbers himself was concerned but advised the Burns-Fry man to use his own judgement, to do what he thought was right, and Lumbers would have a word with Gordon. Lumbers had always affectionally called Gordon "Crotch," but he soon changed this to "Bash" Gordon from the literary character "Bet A Billion Bashby" who was always losing money. And "Bash" Gordon was certainly doing that.

A REPRIEVE FROM SHAKESPEARE

By the end of 1964, Gordon's Montreal era was coming to a close. Gardner Trailers was finally closed down and the assets sold to pay off creditors. The house on Lexington was gone, and Billie and Crawford were living beyond their means in the south of France while maintaining the apartment in Montreal. What net worth the man had when he arrived in Montreal had mostly evaporated. Alimony payments to Mary had virtually stopped. "Why should I continue to pay her now that she's got a job," he would moan to his son Crawford.[26]

"This story would have ended with Crawford ending up on poverty row," recalls stepson Stephen, "if Henry Shakespeare hadn't offered him a job."[27]

The Shakespeare Company of Kalamazoo, Michigan was an internationally renowned producer of recreational products including fishing tackle, archery and golf equipment. Through a number of subsidiaries, the firm also manufactured a broad line of industrial products such as automotive and aircraft parts and controls, fiberglass products for public utilities and other diversified items.

"Crawford had met Henry in Europe," recalls Stephen, "who offered him the position of president and CEO. He took the job, quite frankly because he needed the money."[28] Upon his appointment the Shakespeare Company newsletter explained what Gordon had been doing since leaving A. V. Roe in 1959 by saying he had been in semi-retirement but active in business and government affairs.

"So my mother and Crawford sold the villa in France, took a loss, and moved to a modest little bungalow in Kalamazoo, Michigan in the summer of 1965," recalls stepson Stephen. "Billie, as you can well imagine, was not thrilled with living in Kalamazoo, but she really loved Crawford and felt this was the opportunity he needed to turn himself around."[29] Crawford was not entirely thrilled with the prospect either, revealing to friends that the job was a "step down" from what he had been used to at A. V. Roe. He needn't have worried, for within six months he was fired by the very man that hired him, Henry Shakespeare.

"He lost his job due to drink," recalls his wife Billie. "He just wasn't showing up for work every time when he should. I didn't mind living in Kalamazoo really, 'come downs' in life don't bother me. I've had the best and I can adjust to anything."[30]

With no job, nowhere to go and little money, Billie and Crawford returned to New York and took an apartment on East 62nd Street, a couple of doors away from where Billie and her son Stephen had lived after her divorce in 1947. The apartment was unpretentious and furnished inexpensively, but Billie's flair for decorating made it a home.

"After Shakespeare he was a beaten man," recalls Billie. "He had the capacity; he wanted to go on but it wasn't there. He couldn't. He was on a cloud of his own."[31]

THE CRASH LANDING

By the summer of 1966, Gordon's $3 million had evaporated to just a few thousand dollars. Billie still had some money from her first marriage but not much. Within five years, Gordon had bought and lost two companies, two exclusive homes, one CEO position and most of their physical assets.

Later that summer, an extraordinary episode illustrated Gordon's plight.

On a visit to New York that summer to visit my mother and Crawford, recalls stepson Stephen, he says to us: 'Come with me I want to show you something.' The three of us walk around the corner from the apartment to a tiny jewellery store in the Carlton Hotel. Crawford says: 'Have you got it?' to the jeweller. He gives Crawford a box and in it is the most beautiful pear-shaped diamond ring. He puts it on my mother's finger and she puts her arms around him and she kisses him and she has tears in her eyes. They really did love each other.

Then on the way back to the apartment Billie forgets to buy strawberries for dinner so Crawford tells her to go to a little grocery nearby. Billie refuses, saying they charge too much and at that point Crawford goes ballistic. He's just paid thousands for a ring and my mother insists on walking three blocks to save 90 cents for a basket of strawberries.[32]

By December 1966, most of the Gordon's money had run out. He borrowed $5,000 to keep them going until "things turn around" but needed Billie's co-signature on the loan, her alimony payments as the collateral. At one point he couldn't even raise $200 to send to his daughter Diana travelling in Europe who needed money to get home.

By this time Gordon appeared obsessed, constantly rambling on to family and friends about "turning things around." His son Crawford recalls:

I received a letter from him in early December and it made me really worried. I got the firm I was working for at the time to send me to New York to deliver some documents and we ended up going out for the evening to the 21 Club, a place of special memories for him. It made him happy to see me. Here I was with a degree in business, my CA and working in the business community he loved so much.

He told me he was up for a senior position with a company in Connecticut and that he was one of two people up for consideration and that he was going to get the job and come back and show everyone. I knew it wasn't in the cards for him any more. I knew he wasn't going to get the job. It was sad for me to hear him talk like this and on a number of occasions I had to fight back the tears.[33]

He didn't, in fact, get the job, and he would never get the chance to show anyone, any more. It was the last time he would see his son Crawford.

DROWNING IN DESPAIR

During his Montreal and New York years Gordon seldom talked about his life before Billie. For the most part, Montreal and New York were supposed to be whole new beginnings, fresh starts with fresh faces — except for two things: alcohol and Audrey. Late at night, always after midnight and after quite a few drinks, Gordon would often leave his apartment, and take a cab to Audrey's door, much to her disgust and disappointment. She would complain to a close friend in Toronto, "I just hate that he does this but I can't turn him away. What would he do? Where would he go? I just can't desert him."[34]

As Christmas 1966 approached Gordon grew more and more despondent. He was drinking more heavily — much more heavily. Since leaving A.V. Roe he had been hospitalized twice for serious liver disorders. In the mid-fifties Gordon had admitted himself to the Mayo Clinic to dry out and for the first few weeks back on the job, it looked like he had the problem licked. But the pressure soon got to him and before long he began to have a drink to end a painful day, which led to another and another, quickly reversing the effects of the clinic.

Alcoholism has often been referred to as the disease of denial. Alcoholics rarely admit to themselves that they have the disease, or they minimize it, dismissing it as just heavy drinking. They construct elaborate belief systems to defend themselves against the realization that they are not in control of their drinking any more — it is in control of them.

Gordon faced an additional problem because of his powerful personality and high intelligence. Alcoholics who are former senior executives, and especially those with high intelligence, pose a special dilemma for those trying to treat them. These people create a more elaborate system of alibis than the guy on skid row. They can't accept they're in a situation they can't control; they can't accept they are incapable of stifling their desire for alcohol but because their body has so adapted to alcohol, they cannot function without it. Such was Crawford Gordon during the Christmas season of 1966.

"He would never drink when we went out," recalls his wife Billie. "He was all right in public. He did all of his drinking at home."[35] As Gordon became more and more distraught, Billie became more and more despondent. Her son Stephen was still living in Montreal and once the holidays were over, Billie decided to visit him for a few days. Leaving Crawford alone in the apartment, Billie took the train to Montreal on January 21, 1967 to be with Stephen.

> My mother asked me for advice twice in my life, recalls Stephen. Once before she married Crawford and it was about his drinking and now she was considering divorcing him and it was about his drinking.
>
> My mother felt she hadn't helped him. By divorcing him — and it wasn't because she didn't love him — she hoped he would pull himself together.[36]

Billie decided to ask Crawford for a divorce when she returned to New York the following Thursday, January 26, 1967. She never got the chance.

Chapter Seven

THE FINAL BALE OUT

*E*ven before the scent of her perfume had left the room, the first glass of Scotch was half finished. "I shan't be more than a few days," Billie said when she left. "I'll call you when I get to Montreal." The tall face-worn man, who hated to be alone, was alone. And tired. He had just turned 52, but felt 82.

At just before midnight on Wednesday, January 25, he called his doctor who immediately got an ambulance to rush Gordon to hospital. Soon afterward, Billie was called in Montreal and informed of her husband's condition. A winter storm prevented her from flying home right away so she took the train arriving in New York the next day. When she got to the hospital, Crawford Gordon, industrialist, just turned 52, had already died. Returning to the apartment with a pocketful of his personal effects, she lay down on the sofa and quietly cried herself to sleep.

When the obituary hit the press the next day, reaction was mixed, partly because so many people thought Gordon was already dead years before, having virtually passed out of sight since leaving A. V. Roe. *The Toronto Telegram* called him "the dynamo of A. V. Roe," saying the cause of death was undisclosed.

Fred Smye got the news from one of his sons as he now lived out of the country. He immediately called Jim Floyd in Toronto. Billie Gordon called Mary in Toronto and informed her of the news. Mary, in tears, called her son, Crawford who told Cynthia and Diana. "Crawford called me," recalls Diana. "I felt shaken but very sad. There was a lot of upheaval in our family that day. Mom was very sad but she tried to keep everyone together."[1] Late that evening, Jean Taylor received a phone call at her home in Toronto. It was Audrey Underwood calling from New York. "You know Jean," sobbed Audrey into the phone, "this makes me sad … this makes me so very sad."[2]

Ironically, her relationship with Crawford did end on his terms after all.

By any measurement, it was too short a life. And insular at best. Was he narcissistic, as some people thought, someone who turned inward for gratification and who learned to rely on himself rather than others for safety and self-esteem? Weakness and dependency are threatening to matters of personal adequacy, power, prestige, and status and superiority is always an unconscious priority.

There are signs of this condition in Crawford Gordon.[3] Distanced, abandoned almost, by his parents from a very early age, sent off to private schools in Jamaica and Canada, then to find comfort in a person his parents approved of, a headmaster at Appleby College. From day one Gordon appears to have not been loved as a person in his own right or been provided with any emotional acceptance as a child or an authentic sense of self.

Analysts have felt for years that children who are unable to idealise their parents because of parental indifference or rejection feel devastated, depressed and empty. Through adulthood, they tend to seek idealised parent surrogates who sometimes fail to live up, making them feel even more insular. John Guest, most certainly C.D. Howe, and to some extent Sir Roy Dobson were Gordon's surrogates. They were not successful replacements. Crawford abandoned Guest and then Dobson abandoned him. Even after the magic war years with C.D. Howe, the man he most admired, little was shared between the two men — an occasional phone call or letter, nothing more.

One imagines the few times he was allowed to visit his parents, the sense of loneliness in that home setting probably drove him to become self-involved, to find compensation in achievements and acclaim. This was first demonstrated when Gordon threw himself into school life after his full year of illness at Appleby. His over-achieving lasted through his years with Howe and did not end until the cancellation of the Arrow. And, on that February day in 1959, it was Gordon who was cancelled along with the Arrow.

Narcissistic individuals who are talented have sustained periods of success in their lives, but they never develop the inner skills necessary to regulate their impulses adequately, to channel their needs skilfully or to acquire strategies for resolving conflicts, overcoming failures or regaining a genuine sense of competence after problematic experiences. One could ask if Gordon would have handled the Howard Hughes or John Diefenbaker confrontations differently or could have bounced back after 1959 if those skills were in place. Did alcohol somehow impair those skills?

And what of his relationships — his friendships both male and female? Narcissistic people tend to have shallow emotional lives. They experience little empathy for the feelings of others, they get very little enjoyment from life other than from the tributes they receive from others or from their own grandiose fantasies and they feel restless or bored when external glitter wears off and no new sources feed their self-regard. In general their relationships with other people are exploitive and sometimes parasitic. It is as if they feel they have the right to control and possess others and to exploit them without guilt feelings. Behind a surface which is very often charming and engaging, one senses coldness and ruthlessness. Gordon's own son had concerns about his father's ability to cultivate friendship. And, on more than one occasion, employees were dismissed immediately, ruthlessly and without explanation. Even at the height of the Arrow program, when Gordon should have been firmly at the helm, he vacationed frequently in Europe. Had the glitter of the Arrow not been bright enough for him?

There were three women in his life, two of whom he married. Narcissists frequently select a dependent mate who will be obedient, solicitous and subservient, people who will not expect anything in return except strength and assurances of fidelity. In Mary Gordon he found a woman whose only goal in life was family. In Billie Gordon, he found a woman whose life had rarely moved beyond that of a café society lifestyle. Both women were happy with their lot, happy to be with him and, even despite him, happy. The one woman he couldn't have was Audrey Underwood. It was she who left him and continued to leave him for the rest of his days. The one thing, probably the only thing, he couldn't have, was half his size and twice his strength.

His life touched greatness on more than one occasion. But after 1959 could he really have come back? He always thought so, but he probably, in his heart of hearts, never really believed so. And this is where the sadness begins. His friends knew it; his family knew it; the people that loved him knew it; even the people who hated him knew it. He was someone with greatness in their eyes, yet sadness in his heart.

Even in his final hours, his final moments, the fight was still there. Alone in his apartment that last night, full of alcohol, he didn't want to go just yet, but the choice was no longer his, despite a last frantic phone call to get medical attention. But that night, that cold January night in 1967, perhaps the sadness was too deep, the loneliness too strong and the alcohol too much. Even for him. If it hadn't happened that night, it surely would have another. And with it came the peace that eluded him.

STEPHEN RAPHAEL

I loved Crawford from day one. Because the relationship with my own father really developed later in life, Crawford was the first man who treated me as a person who might have some kind of mind. He's the closest I ever got to having a conventional father. Funny, he used to always tell me not to be a young man in a hurry, not to be too ambitious but to only go when you've got a solid grounding in what you're pursuing. He was someone who wanted his kids to get ahead and amount to something. Our relationship was warm and angry sometimes but highly emotionally charged. He didn't really know how to be a parent. We just found each other ... I needed him and he needed me.

BILLIE GORDON

He was a most generous man and a most attractive individual. My life with Crawford was full of life and fun. It was wonderful, we were very happy. It was difficult in the end, rather pathetic when he got too drunk. He was never abusive or violent and we didn't row or anything. I'm very adaptable. That's why I could by nature stand him as he was, but it was sad to watch in the end. We were very happy for a long time....

DIANA GORDON

I remember warmth, humour and a sense of fun. He demanded your personal best all the time and with integrity. Always go after what you want and don't whine about it. He knew it was a male-dominated world but he always pushed my sister and me. I was always in awe of him. I always felt he was full of love but he didn't know quite how to show it. I don't think he had a lot of confidence in people; he was very insecure with people. When he spent time with us it was very much quality time. We weren't a family that laughed easily but he made us laugh. He was a complex bundle of love and with humour, and he could laugh at himself. He tried to instil character in us. I couldn't understand why I had to spend my summers working in a bank when we didn't need the money. We were never spoiled by him. Having character was very important. We had to go after something because nothing was going to have any meaning for us if we didn't. He gave us things he didn't know he had....

CRAWFORD GORDON III

Although Dad pushed me into just about everything when I was young — golf, tennis etc. — I never worried about being smothered by him. I went about my business politely and I knew he would fall into line eventually. He always wanted me to work for him. "I love you Dad but I can't work for you," I would tell him on more than one occasion. We three kids felt obligated to stand by our mother and if we had to choose between him or her, it was no contest. Not that we loved one more than the other, but it was him that created the divorce. Cynthia had my father's stubbornness; Diana and I have our mother's relaxed qualities. He was charismatic, dynamic yet mercurial. He could dominate a room when he walked in. And yet he was very insecure; he had little confidence in himself, especially after A. V. Roe. He was a business genius and he got things done in a hurry in such a way that Canadians weren't used to at the time. He was one of the great industrialists to come out of this country, but he could have been a lot better.

The funeral was held in New York City over the weekend of January 28, 1967 with some 20 people in attendance, mostly friends of Billie's. Only Gordon's son Crawford and his wife, his daughter Diana and his old friend Len Lumbers came from Toronto for the ceremony. "I couldn't contain myself," recalls Billie Gordon. "I knelt down by the coffin during most of the ceremony. When the service was over I kissed the coffin, said goodbye and walked away." The few people in attendance then returned to Billie's apartment for a few drinks, said their goodbyes and went home. Most would never see, let alone talk to, each other again.

Gordon was cremated, yet to this day no one knows the final resting place of his ashes. Not friends, not family. No one. And so, in death he remains, much as he did in life — alone.

POSTSCRIPT

A.V. ROE CANADA

A. V. Roe never recovered after the collapse of the Arrow and the departure of Crawford Gordon. It struggled along after 1959 with some CF 100 overhaul projects and eventually ended up producing aluminum boats for public and commercial use. A. V. Roe dissolved as a company and was taken over by its parent Hawker-Siddeley on April 30, 1962. Its subsidiaries, like Dosco, were broken up or sold off. Depending on the source one reads, 40,000 or so people, in addition to those laid off at Avro and Orenda, lost their jobs in the aftermath.

None of A.V. Roe's original board of directors are still alive and only two of the original management committee members are still with us: Joe Morley who headed up the company's Sales and Service Division and Bill Dickie, former head of Industrial Relations. From Avro Aircraft Ltd., only Don Rogers who ran flight tests and Jim Floyd who headed up engineering are still alive. With Orenda Engines, only Paul Dilworth, the former chief engineer when it was still called the Gas Turbine Division, is still with us. Of the 30 executives who made up the A.V. Roe Canada management group, only the five remain.

As for the Arrow, the six completed and five near-completed copies of the plane were tendered by War Assets Ltd., the Canadian government's disposal agency, and sold to Sam Lax & Co., a scrap dealer from Hamilton, Ontario. Lax was more interested in the tools and jigs than he was in the aircraft themselves, paying about $300,000 for everything. To him, purchasing the planes, as part of the package, was an inconvenience. So, in April, 1959, Sam Lax bought 11 completed and partially completed Arrows for about $2,500 apiece.

BRIARCREST

The company estate of Briarcrest was sold after A. V. Roe dissolved and went through a number of transformations, becoming everything from a private home to a hairdressing school. It looks much today as it did during the 1950s but is now a real estate office. In 1989 the author received a letter from a former A. V. Roe employee who now, coincidentally, is a real estate agent working at the office at Briarcrest. "You wouldn't believe," he wrote, "how the aura of broads and booze still fill these halls."[1]

CHILDHOOD FAMILY

Crawford Gordon Sr. eventually left banking and became chairman of the board of Norwich Union Insurance. He died while on holiday in Prince Edward Island in 1957, after which Ethel Gordon passed away in 1961. They're both buried in Mount Pleasant Cemetery in Toronto. Bill Gordon, Crawford's brother, eventually ended up in the insurance business and despite being the sole inheritor of his father's estate, never really got into a business that took hold. Despite his chagrin at not receiving any of the inheritance, Crawford "watched out for Bill"[2] until his death in 1962.

OLD FRIENDS

Of all of Crawford's old friends, only Bill Dickie, A. V. Roe's former head of Industrial Relations, is still alive. At 91, he lives near Baysville, Ontario. Len Lumbers, Gordon's closest friend, passed away in December 1995. George Mara, another close friend quoted in this book, is a successful Toronto businessman.

GLORIA COLLINSON

Gloria Collinson was fired from A. V. Roe Canada by the same person who had fired her boss two months earlier, Sir Roy Dobson. Dobson felt that with Gordon gone, Gloria's loyalty would be to her old boss rather than the company. He was right. Collinson later got into advertising and marketing and now owns a successful international marketing company in Toronto. To this day, Collinson says everything she learned about business, she learned from Crawford Gordon. And to this day as well, many people mistake her for Audrey Underwood, Crawford Gordon's *first* secretary.

SIR ROY DOBSON

After the cancellation of the Avro Arrow, Dobson would spend most of his time in England where the British government would treat him much as the Canadian government had done with the Arrow. Years later it would cancel his company's Blue Streak Missile program ironically assembled by another impressive design team. Dobson and Gordon spoke little after the Arrow program. His only contact with the Gordon family was an occasional dinner with Mary Gordon on a rare trip to Canada. Dobson retired as chairman of Hawker-Siddeley in 1967 and died in July of the following year near his home in Sussex. He was 76.

FRED SMYE

After leaving A. V. Roe, Fred Smye bought a small office-supply company, but quickly tired of it and moved to Portugal in the 1970s declaring a "self-imposed exile" from Canada. Smye never got over the Arrow program, always referring to the plane and the company as "his life." When he walked away from Malton in 1959, he vowed "never to set foot on the property again," but he did return when he played a prominent role in the 1979 CBC film, *There Never Was An Arrow.* A. V. Roe Canada's first employee died of cancer in Portugal in December 1985 at age 69.

JIM FLOYD

After the Arrow, Jim Floyd returned to England and worked with a number of Hawker-Siddeley and ex-Avro engineers on several feasibility studies, one of which ended up becoming the Concorde. In 1962 he formed his own aviation consulting company. In 1980, he retired and returned to Canada. Far from retiring, this icon of aviation has continued to contribute to our knowledge of flight, dedicating himself to teaching young people about aircraft and aviation in general. Much sought after by aviation buffs worldwide, he currently lives in Toronto's west end. Crawford Gordon used to tell people he only ever really admired two people in his life. The first was his mentor, C.D. Howe; the second was Jim Floyd.

AUDREY M. UNDERWOOD

After leaving A. V. Roe in 1952, Audrey moved with her family to Sherman Oaks, California and then to New York City where she worked in the travel business. In 1967, only after Crawford Gordon had died, she married her boss to become Mrs. Audrey Newburger and lived in New York for a short time before moving to Florida. In 1972, after her older sister died unexpectedly in Sherman Oaks, Audrey went to the funeral and took care of her sister's children for a short time. One night a next door neighbour shot at a suspected prowler, the bullet ricocheted and struck Audrey, who was standing innocently in her sister's living room. She was hit in the head, never regained consciousness, and died in hospital the next day. Her ashes were sent to her husband in Florida. Audrey died childless.

CRAWFORD GORDON'S CHILDREN

Cynthia Gordon had a personality very much like her father. Unfortunately, as is too often the case, this led to conflict, and father and daughter were estranged during his final years. Cynthia died of cancer in May 1974. Diana Gordon lives in Toronto and is a world-class bridge player. Crawford Gordon III has done extremely well in financial circles and is currently the vice-president and director with a major brokerage house in Toronto. He has three children; his oldest son is named Crawford Gordon IV.

MARY GORDON

Mary Gordon went on to become one of the most successful real estate agents in Toronto proving Bert Willoughby's prophecy to be true. She remained as graceful and non-judgemental as ever, and even after her divorce from Crawford in 1959, never uttered an ill word about her former husband. When he married Billie that same year, Mary's only comment to friends was to wonder how Crawford could ever marry anyone who wore high heels with shorts! Mary was pursued by a number of suitors but remained, for the most part, uninterested, happy to have an occasional dinner with Sir Roy Dobson or Wilf Curtis. In the months leading up to her death on June 17, 1984, in private moments, she would tell her children that if she had a chance to live her life all over again, with the exception of losing her Cynthia, she wouldn't change a thing. And she would marry their father all over again. She died as Mrs. Tierney Gordon.

STEPHEN RAPHAEL

Stephen Raphael lives with his second wife Chrystelle in Westmount in Montreal and, like his stepbrother, works in the world of business and finance. Admitting freely that anything he learned about business he learned from his stepfather, Stephen has a passion for Hollywood and the cinema and is currently working on a book about Hollywood musicals.

GABRIELLE "BILLIE" GORDON

Billie never looked back after her husband's funeral. She closed up the apartment in New York and stayed with her son, Stephen, in Montreal for a few weeks before moving back to England. She lives quite comfortably near London with a man she has known for over 20 years. Never remarrying, she still goes by the name of Mrs. Crawford Gordon.

BIBLIOGRAPHY

Avro Newsmagazine, 10th Anniversary Edition, 1955.

Bothwell, Robert and William Kilbourne. *C.D. Howe: A Biography*. Toronto: McClelland and Stewart, 1979.

Davie, Michael. *The Titanic: The Full Story of A Tragedy*. London: The Bodley Head, 1986.

Dow, James. *The Arrow*. Toronto: James Lorimer and Co., 1979.

Earl, Marjorie. "How Roy Dobson Pushed Us Into The Jet Age", *Macleans* magazine, July 20, 1957.

Eayrs, James. *In Defence of Canada: Appeasement and Rearmament*. Toronto: University of Toronto Press, 1965.

Floyd, James C. *The Avro Canada C-102 Jetliner*. Erin, Ontario: Boston Mills Press, 1986.

— "The Avro Story." *Canadian Aviation* 50th Anniversary Issue, 1978.

Frost, Stanley Brice. *McGill University*, Vol. 1. Montreal and Kingston: McGill-Queens University Press, 1980.

Garbet and Goulding. *The Lancaster At War*. Shepperton, England: Ian Allen Ltd., 1971.

Gunston, Bill. *Early Supersonic Fighters of the West*. Shepperton, England: Ian Allen Ltd., 1976.

Harbron, John D. *C. D. Howe*. Toronto: Fitzhenry and Whiteside Ltd., 1980.

Johnston, Archibald F. *Canadian General Electric's First Hundred Years*. Toronto: CGE, 1982.

Newman, Peter C. *The Canadian Establishment: Volume One: The Old Guard*. Toronto: McClelland and Stewart, 1975.

Porter, John. *The Vertical Mosaic: An Analysis of Social Class and Power in Canada*. Toronto: University of Toronto Press, 1965.

Regehr, Ernie. *Making A Killing: Canada's Arms Industry*. Toronto: McClelland and Stewart, 1975.

Roberts, Leslie. *C.D.: The Life and Times of Clarence Decatur Howe*. Toronto: Clarke-Irwin, 1959.

Smith, Denis. *Rogue Tory: The Life and Legend of John G. Diefenbaker*. Toronto: MacFarlane Walter and Ross, 1995.

Sobel, David and Susan Meurer. *Working At Inglis: The Life and Death of a Canadian Factory*. Toronto: James Lorimer and Company, 1994.

Stacey, C. P. *Arms, Men and Governments: The War Policies of Canada, 1939-1945*. Ottawa: Department of National Defence, 1970.

Stewart, Greig. *Shutting Down the National Dream: A.V. Roe and the Tragedy of the Avro Arrow*. Toronto: McGraw-Hill Ryerson, 1988.

Wente, Margaret, ed. *I Never Say Anything Provocative: Witticisms, Anecdotes, and Reflections by Canada's Most Outspoken Politician, John G. Diefenbaker*. Toronto: Peter Martin Associates, 1975.

NOTES

*C*itations in the notes are in abbreviated form. Full references are given in the bibliography. Interviews with people in Crawford Gordon's life form an important part of this book. Listed below are the names and dates of those quoted. The dates listed indicate the date of the first interview with the author. Some people were interviewed on more than one occasion on dates too numerous to list.

INTERVIEWS

Ron Adey August 27, 1979

Anonymous May 12, 1997

Winnet Boyd January 1, 1978

Margaret Brown October 16, 1980

Lou Cahill June 6, 1997

Gloria Collinson April 22, 1997

Paul Dilworth February 13, 1978

John Easton November 25, 1978

Jim Floyd October 6, 1979

Jim Gilmore June 6, 1997

Billie Gordon July 16, 1997

Crawford Gordon III May 21, 1997

Diana Gordon July 24, 1997

Mary Gordon April 13, 1980

David Hahn May 17, 1997

Stan Harper February 9, 1978

Jack Hilton January 2, 1978

Jim Hornick February 12, 1978

Bob Johnson May 10, 1978

Pat Kelly April 14, 1978

George Mara July 21, 1997

Ken Molson March 8, 1979

Joe Morley May 2, 1978

John Pallett July 9, 1979

Stephen Raphael June 21, 1997

Don Rogers October 30, 1978

Joe Schultz November 26, 1978

Dorothy Smye November 22, 1979

Fred Smye April 24, 1979

Jean Taylor July 22, 1997

Tom Thompson June 20, 1997

PROLOGUE

1. Hornick interview.
2. *Canadian Business,* May 22, 1954.
3. Raphael interview and Crawford Gordon III interview.
4. *Canadian Business,* May 22, 1954.

CHAPTER 1: THE EARLY YEARS (1912-36)

1. Davie, *The Titanic,* p. 52.
2. The *Toronto Star,* April 9, 1912.
3. Davie, p. 75.
4. Crawford Gordon III interview.
5. J. Batten, The Appleby Story, Appleby College, 1985, p. 1.
6. J. Murphy to Appleby College August 24, 1925. Appleby Archives.
7. Appleby College For Boys, A Brochure, circa 1927.
8. C. Gordon to J.B. Corbett, July 9, 1927.
9. C. Gordon to J.S.H. Guest, November 4, 1926.
10. Ibid., December 27, 1927.
11. Ibid., November 14, 1929.

12. Ibid., May 29, 1929.

13. Argus Yearbook, Appleby College, February 1930.

14. Appleby College For Boys, A Brochure, circa 1927.

15. Gordon to Guest, March 20, 1931.

16. Ibid., August 31, 1931.

17. Crawford Gordon III interview.

18. Raphael interview.

19. Ibid.

20. Frost, *McGill University*, Vol. 1, p.1.

21. Thompson interview.

22. Raphael interview.

23. "Old McGill 1936", McGill University.

CHAPTER 2: FIRST CAREER MOVES

1. Johnston, *Canadian General Electric's First Hundred Years.*

2. *Canadian Business*, May 22, 1954.

3. Diana Gordon interview.

4. Crawford Gordon III interview.

5. Ibid.

6. Ibid.

7. Mary Gordon interview.

8. Crawford Gordon III interview.

9. Raphael interview.

10. Ibid.

11. *Canadian Business*, May 22, 1954.

12. Harbron, *C.D. Howe*, p. 37.

13. Fred Smye interview.

14. Newman, *The Canadian Establishment*, vol. 1, p. 370.

15. Bothwell and Kilbourn, *C.D. Howe: A Biography*, p. 114.

16. Morley interview.

17. Fred Smye interview.

18. Bothwell and Kilbourn, pp. 4-5.

19. Newman, p. 375.

20. Newman, p. 373.

21. Roberts, *The Life and Times of C.D. Howe*, p. 186.

22. Roberts, p. 5.

23. Eayrs, *In Defence of Canada: Appeasement and Rearmament*, p. 177.

24. Eayrs, p. 134.

25. Stacey, *Arms, Men and Government*.

26. Bothwell and Kilbourn, p. 131.

27. Mary Gordon interview.

28. Newman, p. 359. See also Porter, *The Vertical Mosaic*, p. 430.

29. Roberts, p. 127.

30. Newman, p. 366.

31. Bothwell and Kilbourn, p. 13.

32. Earl, "How Roy Dobson Pushed Us Into the Jet Age".

33. Fred Smye interview.

34. Ibid.

35. Earl article.

36. Ibid.

37. Garbet and Goulding, *The Lancaster at War*, p. 14.

38. Earl article.

39. Newman, p. 358.

40. Fred Smye interview.

41. Harper interview.

42. Hornick interview.

43. Earl article.

44. Ibid.

45. Bothwell and Kilbourn, p. 182.

46. Gordon to Howe, December 12, 1945. Gordon Papers.

47. Howe to Gordon, December 13, 1945. Gordon Papers.

CHAPTER 3: RETURN TO PRIVATE BUSINESS

1. Crawford Gordon III interview.

2. Fred Smye interview.

3. Newman, p. 374.

4. Fred Smye interview.

5. The *Globe and Mail*, October 11, 1945.

6. Ibid., November 30, 1945.

7. *Avro Newsmagazine*, 10th Anniversary Edition , 1955.

8. Crawford Gordon interview.

9. Sobel and Meurer, *Working at Inglis: The Life and Death of a Canadian Factory*, p. 37.

10. Ibid., p. 102.

11. English Electric would build water turbines for the Generating Station at Niagara Falls and those for the Canadian side of the St. Lawrence Seaway.

12. Hahn interview.

13. Ibid.

14. Dobson to Symington, May 19, 1945. Howe Papers.

15. The *Globe and Mail*, July 24, 1945.

16. Molson interview.

17. *Avro Newsmagazine*, 10th Anniversary Edition, 1955.

18. Stewart, *Shutting Down the National Dream: A.V. Roe and the Tragedy of the Avro Arrow*, p. 47.

19. The *Globe and Mail*, October 13, 1945.

20. Earl article.

21. Fred Smye interview.

22. Hahn interview.

23. Cahill interview.

24. Gilmore interview.

25. Hahn interview.

26. Ibid.

27. Johnson interview.

28. Adey interview.

29. Brown interview.

30. Hornick interview.

31. Sobel and Meurer, p. 105.

32. Hahn interview.

CHAPTER 4: RETURN TO OTTAWA: DEPARTMENT OF DEFENCE PRODUCTION AND AVRO'S FIRST PROJECTS (1951)

1. Floyd, "The Avro Story".

2. Jim Bain was born in Edinburough and entered the RAF Engineering College in 1920. He came to Canada in 1938 and joined TCA soon after it was

formed. He became TCA's superintendant of maintenance and overhaul and in 1945 its superintendant of engineering and maintenance. He became known as the father of the famous aircraft, the North Star.

3. *Rochester Democrat and Chronicle*, April 19, 1956.

4. *Avro Newsmagazine*, 10th Anniversary Edition, 1955.

5. Ibid.

6. Floyd interview.

7. The *Globe and Mail*, October 18, 1951.

8. Ibid.

9. Ibid.

10. Schultz interview.

11. Fred Smye interview.

12. Easton interview.

13. Earl article.

14. Fred Smye interview.

15. Bothwell and Kilbourn, p. 257.

16. The *Ottawa Standard*, February 28, 1951.

17. *Time* magazine, October 20, 1951.

18. Ibid. See also *Winnipeg Free Press*, February 28, 1951.

19. *Industry Canada*, July 1951.

20. National Defence College, July 11, 1951.

21. *Montreal Standard*, September 11, 1951.

22. Anonymous interview.

23. Fred Smye interview.

24. House of Commons Debates, April 4, 1952.

25. Crawford Gordon II's speech to the National Defence College, July 11, 1951.

26. Fred Smye interview.

27. Dilworth interview.

28. Adey interview.

29. Fred Smye interview.

CHAPTER 5: A. V. ROE CANADA (1951 - 59)

1. Fred Smye interview.

2. Porter, pp. 430 and 550.

3. Hilton interview.

4. The *Globe and Mail*, October 12, 1951.

5. House of Commons Debates, V, 1955, p. 5379.

6. Adey interview.

7. The *Globe and Mail*, October 12, 1951.

8. *Time* magazine, December 6, 1954.

9. Fred Smye interview.

10. Floyd interview.

11. Howe to Gordon, December 13, 1951. Howe Papers.

12. Boyd interview.

13. Speech to the Canadian Club, March 17, 1957.

14. Ibid.

15. Floyd, p. 107.

16. Collinson interview.

17. Anonymous Interview.

18. Collinson interview.

19. Adey interview.

20. *A.V. Roe Newsletter*, October 1953.

21. Taylor interview.

22. *A.V. Roe Newsletter*, Spring 1952.

23. Floyd, p. 104.

24. The *Globe and Mail*, June 10, 1956. Howe was apparently confused when he made these particular comments. During the jetliner flight tests, water ballast tanks were carried to simulate passenger loads and to test fuel consumption. This "sandbag" comment causes irritation to Avro employees, especially Jim Floyd, even today.

25. Ibid.

26. Floyd interview.

27. Rogers interview.

28. Fred Smye interview.

29. Floyd, p. 116.

30. Ibid., p. 117.

31. Stewart, p. 161.

32. Howe to Gordon, March 5, 1952. Howe Papers.

33. Howe to Gordon, July 26, 1952. Howe Papers.

34. The *Globe and Mail*, January 5, 1952.

35. Easton interview.

36. Ibid.

37. Ibid.

38. *Canadian Aviation Magazine*, 50th Anniversary Edition, 1978.

39. Howe to Claxton, December 9, 1952. Howe Papers.

40. The Toronto *Telegram*, September 25, 1953.

41. Howe to Gordon, July 28, 1953. Howe Papers.

42. Ibid., August 28, 1953. Howe Papers.

43. Hornick interview.

44. Kelly interview.

45. Ibid.

46. Ibid.

47. Ibid.

48. Dorothy Smye interview.

49. Anonymous interview.

50. Ibid.

51. Collinson interview.

52. Anonymous interview.

53. Ibid.

54. The *Globe and Mail*, February 10, 1953.

55. Ibid., January 1, 1954.

56. *Canadian Aviation Magazine*, 50th Anniversary Edition, 1978.

57. The *Globe and Mail*, June 25, 1954.

58. *Canadian Aviation Magazine*, 50th Anniversary Edition, 1978.

59. Ibid.

60. Collinson interview.

61. Fred Smye interview.

62. The *Globe and Mail*, April 17, 1954.

63. Crawford Gordon III interview.

64. The *Globe and Mail*, December 4, 1954.

65. Canadian Manufacturers Association, June 7, 1956.

66. *Montreal Gazette*, March 15, 1955.

67. A.V. Roe Canada 10th Anniversay Dinner Souvenir Book, December 1, 1955.

68. Ibid.

69. Ibid.

70. Dow, *The Arrow*, p. 99.

71. The *Globe and Mail*, January 21, 1957.

72. Ibid., July 16, 1955.

73. Collinson interview.

74. Anonymous interview.

75. Collison interview.

76. Dow, p 100.

77. The *Globe and Mail*, April 21, 1953.

78. The *Toronto Star*, May 24, 1956.

79. Crawford Gordon Papers, May 14, 1958.

80. *Financial Post*, October 2, 1956.

81. Crawford Gordon III interview.

82. Wood Gundy prospectus.

83. Kelly interview.

84. *Avro Newsmagazine*, 10th Anniversary Edition, 1945-55.

85. The *Globe and Mail*, June 10, 1957.

86. Crawford Gordon III interview.

87. Mara interview.

88. Dow, p. 102.

89. Kelly interview.

90. The Toronto *Telegram*, October 10, 1959.

91. The *Globe and Mail*, August 10, 1957.

92. Kelly interview.

93. *Saturday Night* magazine, September 14, 1957.

94. Ibid.

95. Ibid.

96. Ibid.

97. Ibid.

98. *Business Week*, November 16, 1957.

99. Raphael interview.

100. Ibid.

101. Gunston, *Supersonic Fighters of the West*, p. 133.

102. Ibid.

103. Floyd to Author, June 18, 1997.

104. *Business Week*, November 16, 1957.

105. James Eayrs, unpublished manuscript.

106. The *Globe and Mail*, May 9, 1958.

107. Ibid., February 23, 1958.

108. *Canadian Aviation Magazine*, 50th Anniversary Edition, 1978.

109. The *Globe and Mail*, February 21, 1958.

110. A.V. Roe Canada Meeting Minutes, June 8-10, 1958. Author Papers.

111. Ibid.

112. Ibid.

113. Ibid.

114. Smye to O'Hurley, August 7, 1958. Smye Papers.

115. Fred Smye interview.

116. Crawford Gordon III interview.

117. Diana Gordon interview.

118. Crawford Gordon interview.

119. Ibid.

120. Ibid.

121. Pallett interview.

122. Fred Smye interview.

123. The Arrow Program, September 16, 1958. Smye Papers.

124. Kelly interview.

125. Pallett interview.

126. Ibid.

127. Smith, *Rogue Tory*, p. 635.

128. Morley interview.

129. Fred Smye interview.

130. Adey interview.

131. Raphael interview.

132. The *Globe and Mail*, September 24, 1958.

133. Ibid., September 25, 1958.

134. The *Toronto Star*, March 9, 1986.

135. Howe to Pearson, January 22, 1959. Howe Papers.

136. George Hees interviewed by Richard O'Brian, February 20, 1979, CBC TV, Current Affairs.

137. Speech in the House of Commons, February 20, 1959.

138. Ibid.

139. Kelly interview.

140. Fred Smye interview.

141. The *Toronto Star*, February 20, 1959.

142. The *Globe and Mail*, February 21, 1959.

143. Ibid.

144. Ibid.

145. Ibid.

146. The *Toronto Star*, February 23, 1959.

147. The *Globe and Mail*, February 23, 1959.

148. The *Globe and Mail* and The Toronto *Telegram*, February 24, 1959.

149. Harbron, p. 26.

150. The *Ottawa Gazette*, February 26, 1959.

151. Ibid.

152. Ibid.

153. Ibid.

154. Ibid.

155. Collinson interview.

156. "There Never Was An Arrow", George Robertson, producer, CBC, 1978.

157. Morley interview.

158. Dobson to Diefenbaker, June 17, 1959. Collinson Papers.

159. Collinson interview.

160. The *Globe and Mail*, July 2, 1959.

161. Anonymous interview.

CHAPTER 6: THE FINAL YEARS (1959 -67)

1. Raphael interview.

2. Ibid.

3. Ibid.

4. Ibid.

5. Ibid.

6. Billie Gordon interview.

7. Collinson interview.

8. Crawford Gordon III interview.

9. Raphael interview.

10. Billie Gordon interview.

11. Raphael interview.

12. Crawford Gordon III interview.

13. *Financial Post,* June 11, 1960.

14. Raphael interview.

15. Billie Gordon interview.

16. Crawford Gordon III interview.

17. Raphael interview.

18. Ibid.

19. Mara interview.

20. Raphael interview.

21. Ibid.

22. Ibid.

23. Crawford Gordon III interview.

24. Raphael interview.

25. Ibid.

26. Crawford Gordon III interview.

27. Raphael interview.

28. Ibid.

29. Ibid.

30. Billie Gordon interview.

31. Ibid.

32. Raphael interview.

33. Crawford Gordon III interview.

34. Anonymous interview.

35. Billie Gordon interview.

36. Raphael interview.

CHAPTER 7: THE FINAL BALE OUT (1967)

1. Diana Gordon interview.

2. Taylor interview.

3. This diagnosis and the following analysis of Crawford Gordon's personality are based on discussions with a psychiatrist, Dr. Wilson Gasewicz.

POSTSCRIPT

1. Letter from Geoff Grossmith, January 31, 1989.
2. Crawford Gordon III interview.

PHOTO CREDITS

Karsh Portrait: Courtesy Gordon Family

Crawford Gordon at 7: Courtesy Gordon Family

Crawford Gordon at 11: Courtesy Gordon Family

Crawford Gordon at 21: Courtesy Gordon Family

Appleby College Football Team 1930: Courtesy Appleby College Alumni Relations

20-Year-Old Mary Tierney: Courtesy Diana Gordon

Tierney Women 1920: Courtesy Gordon Family

Tierney/Gordon Wedding, September 1936: Courtesy Gordon Family

Four Key Players 1958: Courtesy Jim Floyd

Orenda Engines Plant Tour, September 1952: Courtesy National Aviation Museum

CF-100 Enters Squadron Use — Late 1950s: Courtesy Author's Collection

Avro C-102 Jetliner Flying Over New York City on April 18, 1950: Barrie artist Bill Heap's painting. Courtesy Author's Collection

The Production Line: Courtesy National Aviation Museum and Orenda Aerospace Corporation

King Edward Hotel, 1957: Courtesy Gordon Family

12-Year-Old Cynthia Gordon Assists Her Father: Courtesy Gordon Family

Arrow Roll-Out, October 4, 1957: Courtesy Gordon Family

Three Giants at the Arrow Roll-Out on October 4, 1957: Courtesy Jim Floyd

Autumn 1958: Courtesy Author's Collection

Billie Raphael, 1942 Hollywood: Courtesy Stephen Raphael

Crawford and Billie on Their Honeymoon, July 1959: Courtesy Stephen Raphael

19-Year-Old Billie Raphael (1941): Courtesy Stephen Raphael

Westmount Estate, Summer 1960: Courtesy Stephen Raphael

Summer 1960: Courtesy Stephen Raphael

Partying at Maxim's in Paris, 1961: Courtesy Stephen Raphael

March 25, 1958, First Flight of Arrow RL-201: Courtesy Author's Collection and Hawker-Siddeley

INDEX

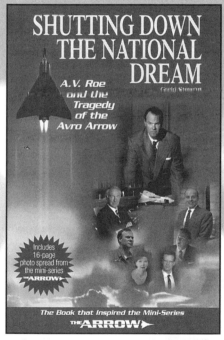